ON THE Yellow Brick Road

On the Yellow Brick Road

My Search for Home and Hope for the Child with Autism

ISBN: 978-0-9993135-0-3 U.S.A.

Published by Offerings Publishing, Novato, CA.

Photograph, back cover: Pilar Espana
Cover and book design: Gilman Design, Larkspur, CA

ON THE Yellow Brick Road

Karen Kaplan

*To my very own wizard, Max Kaplan, a father who believed
I had the brains, heart, and courage to do whatever I dreamed,
and to my fairy god-brother, Darryl Kaplan, who watched over
me after we lost our father.*

*And to the three munchkins, Joshua, Sean, and Tyler,
my three sons who show me where my home truly resides.*

Acknowledgments

Thank you, Dad, for believing in me and teaching me that anything is possible if I gained knowledge and experience and was not afraid to ask.

Thank you, Joshua, Sean, and Tyler, for believing your mom had an important story to share. You are my home.

Agnes Liebhardt, thank you for helping me think about living my passion and purpose in a bigger way.

Thank you, Lawrence Furman, for acknowledging that I, too, had a book inside me and for encouraging me to just sit down and write it.

Thank you, Laura Shumaker, for reading a bit of the story and encouraging me to write more.

Thank you, Laura Briggin, for taking your valuable time to read this story and offer your amazing positive smile and winks, encouraging me to move forward.

Thank you, my dear friend Meg Affinito, for listening to pieces of my story and inspiring me to put my life into words. Thank you for being my friend and sharing your very special son with me on my road with autism.

Thank you, Jim Baldwin, for all your helpful editing, enabling me to express my journey in a clear and compelling manner. Thank you, David Sweet, for putting the final touches on the written word.

Thank you, Jacqueline Gilman, for reading, listening, and connecting to my words in order to design the important package that embraces my story.

A special note of gratitude to Helen, Barry, Susan, and Rusty for being the first children to arouse my curiosity in children who communicate differently, which led to an extreme interest and then a passion for helping those with unique abilities.

CONTENTS

Stories

Appendix

Foreward

THE JOY OF A NEW soul coming into my life quickly turned to devastation with the diagnosis of autism. During the '70s, the diagnosis of a child with autism offered no hope, no education, no programs, or even a book to read to give you hope. Professionals offered you a bleak future: the institution. Everywhere you turned, day care, friends, family, and doctors gave the same familiar advice: institutionalize and move on. Parents were pretty much left on their own to figure things out.

In the midst of this dark hole in my life, unwilling to give up on my son, I kept searching for help. I met Karen Kaplan when my son was four. She was so positive and inspirational. It was the first time in four years I had heard anyone express hope. Karen talked to me as though my son could be educated despite his diagnosis. An institution was never an option for Karen. For me, though, it was a high price. Karen was opening a residential program two hours away; thus, my son would go there to live. I would have to trust someone I didn't know to give me the help no one else I knew could offer. I had to give up so much to save my sweet son.

As the years went by, I grew to trust and love Karen. I watched Kyle learn, experience, trust, and let others into his life. He learned to swim, play, and get along with others. It was not an easy journey, but it saved my son in his growing years. This part of the journey gave me hope that, despite his affliction, he could eventually live a good life away from an institution. He spent eighteen years of his life under Karen's guidance. When she lost the Kaplan Foundation, Kyle, Karen, and I all left together. As hard as it was to leave the Kaplan Foundation, I knew my son had solid groundwork to move on to the next season of his life. Karen's tutelage focused on independent living. Kyle now lives with a roommate, goes to work, and enjoys as normal a life as possible. He has friends, which is the greatest accomplishment of all.

Although his journey still continues with all the ups and downs of life, it is still very hard for me. What I have learned, what I embrace with all my heart, is to never give up hope. No matter how bad things get, and they do now and then, I know not to give up hope. I long for the safe days at the Kaplan Foundation but I am so grateful to have had even one day there. The experience for my son and me was absolutely unforgettable.

Today, Karen is the best friend I have ever had. Her journey became my own, and now my son is in his forties and does okay. The trials and tribulations I have gone through by no means have been easy. I am very thankful to have had eighteen years of great knowledge to guide me.

~ Meg Affinito, mom and friend

Preface

My journey from babysitting to directing schools
and why I wrote this book

I WROTE THIS BOOK TO offer some sense of connection to all those who are affected by the world of autism, to inspire, but most of all to bring hope.

It is about my forty years of experience with autism. It is about my inner journey during these forty years. It's about overcoming obstacles, finding our true passion, and reaching a place where we feel most at home.

When I turned sixty-five I wondered more deeply than ever before what my legacy might be and realized it was my experience with autism. With the encouragement and the energy of those who believed I had something to share and the anger aroused in me by the author of *Far from the Tree*, the book was born.

I don't know the exact year I decided that I, too, should write a book about autism, but it had been on my mind since I moved from the Sacramento area to Marin County, about fifteen years ago.

I thought about writing *Reach Me Teach Me Too*, a sequel to *Reach Me Teach Me*, my first published handbook, guiding teachers in public school settings to develop programs for children with autism. I thought about it again when I was teaching at the universities and again as I unpacked the autism quilt, given to me by parents whose children attended my first private school in Orangevale, California. I thought I might just tell the stories of the children and their families showcased on the fifty-two squares of that quilt.

But it wasn't until a very specific series of events, occurring over the last four years, that I finally lit my candle calling in my writing guides, as suggested by Lawrence Furman, author of *Memoir of a Slightly Mad Mystic,* and sat down and just wrote. I had met Lawrence once for a brainstorming session at Whole Foods in Novato, California, and he helped me to see the possibility and acknowledged that I, too, had a story worth sharing.

Agnes, one of my key mentors, had laid the foundation a couple of years prior. She suggested that I "Think Bigger" and embrace my abilities to teach and help others. There was also my very angry read of *Far from the Tree* that occurred just before my meeting Lawrence and that added necessary fuel.

Lawrence gave me my first piece of advice as a writer: "When you ask anyone to read your work, only ask them what they enjoyed." I did share a few of my pieces with a colleague or two and with a mother of a child with autism. They all encouraged me to continue.

It was Lawrence again who connected me to my first editor and he, in turn, to a book designer.

I wrote, he edited. I rewrote, he edited. I clarified. I moved pieces around to make the flow seem smoother. I came up with section titles. I imagined the book cover and the title and learned the function of the preface, foreword, and epilogue and decided a glossary of terms wasn't needed.

I remember thinking my mother would be astonished that I was writing a book. The child who always received comments like "improvement needed in handwriting, spelling, and grammar" on her report card was really writing a book.

I observed how my editor reversed sentence format to strengthen the story's impact and how he suggested leaving out words that made little difference to the meaning. I found that I enjoyed writing. I liked finding just the right words and exploring ways I could have the reader feel emotions and visualize the situation a child, family, or I was in.

So, I wrote and I wrote and I wrote every chance I had, often four to eight hours at a sitting, for nearly a year. It finally came together. There was actually a journey of hope unfolding and being shared and a beginning and an ending materializing.

I smiled, I cried, I remembered, and finally I just imagined how my story might offer a sense of connection, inspiration, and hopefulness.

If you are a parent of a child with autism, my hope is that you will gain at least one new idea for taking care of yourself, one new idea for helping your loved one with autism, and also develop a greater sense that you are not alone. If you are a professional in the field of autism, my hope is that you will understand the parent's perspective a little better, be inspired to never give up, see capabilities, find your true passion, and leave a legacy.

Finally, my hope is that everyone who reads this book realizes that their life is a journey with forks in the road, and that it is the choices we make at those forks and with those we meet along the way that bring us to the home we desire. As Dorothy said in *The Wizard of Oz*, "There's no place like home."

Introduction

EVERY PROGRAM MUST HAVE A beginning. Sacramento City Schools had decided to open its first public school program for children with autism. I would be its first teacher.

Early one day I arrived at Napa State Hospital, ready to meet Mary, a child with autism who would soon be leaving the hospital and joining my class. I was greeted by the ward staff, who told me to be sure to keep my distance from Mary. She was prone to grabbing, pulling out her own hair, and screaming when she was anxious. I remember, walking in, the coldness of the place and its medicinal smell. There were no colors, just a grayness. The corridors echoed as I approached the final door to Mary's unit. Inside, children were walking around aimlessly. No activities were going on. All toys, games, and equipment appeared to be locked in large metal cabinets, secured to the walls. The staff hovered around the office area. No one seemed interested in engaging with these children.

One of the staff brought Mary to me. She had a shaggy, brown rag stuffed in her mouth, with many inches of it hanging down over her chin and neck. Her eyes were wide open and looked straight back at me. She was pale, but her eyes were very expressive. The staff introduced me and I greeted her, holding out my hand. I said, "Mary, I am Karen. I am glad to meet you. Can you take me to your room and show me around?" Mary reached for my hand and that was it. Mary and I began our relationship.

About thirty days later, when Mary stepped off the yellow school bus to attend Clayton B. Wire Elementary School, I again extended my hand. I explained to Mary she could not have a rag in her mouth at school. I knew that it was important to start new expectations right away with children with autism. If I allowed Mary to continue to hold that rag in her mouth in this new environment, destroying her teeth and impairing her ability to communicate with others, there would be a longer process ahead of me in changing this behavior.

Mary took the rag out of her mouth that day, and with a long sigh of relief and a great deal of hope, I began her teaching. She never put anything back in her mouth again.

Mary is just one child whose life has touched mine. Her story and the stories of many other children with autism I have come to know have helped me see that my favorite childhood film, *The Wizard of Oz*, somehow helps me to understand my journey of forty years. My journey has been about gaining knowledge the Scarecrow knew he needed to solve important problems, about using heart to guide me like the Tin Man and building courage like the Cowardly Lion. Perhaps I relate most to Dorothy because, unknown to me then, I shared a similar desire to find home and to uncover the power of my own Ruby Slippers.

So, imagine securing some type of ruby shoes to your feet (boots, high-tops, Mary Janes, stilettos) and walk with me. Perhaps something on my road will help you find hope and your own way home.

The Last Push

I DON'T RECALL WHAT PUSHED me to search Amazon for *Far from the Tree*, by Mr. Andrew Solomon, but it must have been predestined, because I ended up with two copies of that book—one hardbound and the other paper. This book that beckoned me was the thickest book I had attempted to read in some time. It was filled with pages addressing a wide variety of special needs topics, such as Down syndrome, schizophrenia, and, of course, autism.

My mission: to rip into the chapter on autism and come away with some remarkable tidbits that would continue to help me on my road to understanding and addressing autism. I never truly expected what happened next.

As with many books on the subject, there were the heartfelt stories from parents raising children on the spectrum. The stories were moving and helped the reader understand who these children were, what their parents were going through emotionally, and how the fields of medicine, science, education, and therapy were helping to provide answers. Up to that point I thought, "Well done, Mr. Solomon. Nicely staged, nicely integrated, and somewhat hopeful."

The author then elected to tell stories of mothers or fathers who had chosen to end the lives of their child with autism, and sometimes their own in the process. He asked why these parents should be given lesser punishments for taking the lives of their children than any other murderer. He concluded that the system is devaluing the lives of these children.

I couldn't believe I had wasted my valuable time reading this man's work. I felt so many troubling thoughts and emotions stirring inside. The strongest was anger. Why would he choose this approach? What was he thinking? Why couldn't he have chosen to end with a statement about how far we had come in research and intervention? Did he truly not understand the despair these families were feeling? And why in God's name would he choose to pour salt on the parents' wounds by arguing that a lesser punishment was unjust and indicated that society did not value the lives of these children as much as the lives of others?

My chest was heavy, my mind dark. Then, as so often happens (thank goodness), I saw everything in a different light. "Okay, Mr. Solomon," I thought. "You don't want me to become complacent. You want me to continue to question my naive thinking that, over the past forty years, we have come a long way. Even if we have acquired more knowledge, more understanding, and more resources than ever before, we have not yet reached the Emerald City. Perhaps I must travel further on this road before I can enter the gates and find my way home."

Mr. Solomon, I must give you credit. Thank you for giving me the push I seemed to require. I must have needed stronger motivation to move forward. Perhaps now is the time to write the story I have started many times before. Now I am ready to sit down and write a story that could provide hope through knowledge, heart, and courage. I have more reason that ever before. Thank you, Mr. Andrew Solomon.

For as long as parents see no solution but to end their son's or daughter's life, I am in no position to click my Ruby Slippers three times and leave the Land of Oz. I have not truly found home.

The Film That Started It All

I BELIEVE MY JOURNEY ON the road to meeting autism started when I was nine years old. My mother took me to see the film *The Miracle Worker*, the story of Helen Keller and her teacher, Annie Sullivan. So many scenes in the film grabbed hold of my heart and started my quest to become someone just like Annie Sullivan, Helen's teacher.

One of those moving scenes was at the dining room table. Helen had always been allowed to circle the table while her family enjoyed their meal together. Her teacher, Annie Sullivan, is so disappointed with the family for allowing their daughter to feed like an animal, eating off each of their plates, using her hands, and stuffing her face.

Annie can't stand it. She believes in Helen's capability. She knows in her mind and in her heart that Helen can be taught. She asks the family to leave the room to allow her to help Helen learn to sit at a table and eat with a proper utensil. With much anxiety, the family leaves and Annie gets into the most tiring battle of wits with Helen. Food is flying, forks are flying, and chairs are knocked down. But in the end, Helen is sitting at the table using her spoon like one of the family. Her teacher, Annie, covered in food, hair all out of place, and her spectacles nearly broken, feels a great sense of pride.

The final scene in this film takes place outside in the family's garden. Annie has been working for months to help Helen learn that everything has a name. Annie finger-spells every object in Helen's world into her hands, while having Helen also experience the object through taste, touch, and smell.

Helen is at the water pump, pushing hard to force the water out of the pump and into her hands for a drink. Annie intervenes and doesn't allow Helen to have the water until she spells the word, water, into Annie's hand. For me, the most exciting moment in the film came when Helen spells out W-A-T-E-R. Helen finally realizes that things have names and that if she can learn these names and use them, the whole world can open up to her. Like me in the theater that day, Annie is breathless. She knows she has opened the world up to Helen. She sees finally that Helen is hungry to understand her world and engage in it.

By the end of the film, I knew that I wanted to develop the knowledge, heart, and courage that Annie Sullivan possessed. I knew I wanted to help children with such challenges learn to communicate with the world. Annie Sullivan was my first mentor.

Building My Brains
and Gaining Experience

IN MIDDLE SCHOOL, I BECAME a babysitter for two deaf-mute children who lived across the street. I was able to observe their sessions with professionals who were helping them learn to communicate. By the time I was in high school, I had researched the profession of speech therapy, and subsequently applied to Arizona State University, which had a great reputation in preparing students to become speech therapists.

One of the expectations of my college program was that I meet the 500 clinical hours of working with a variety of speech and language cases in the clinic. This is where I met Rusty and his mom, Charlene. Rusty was my first experience working with a child with autism.

This was the early 1970s, and none of my professors at that time had much experience working with children with autism. So they encouraged me to research on my own to try to help Rusty and his mother in any way I felt might work. So that is what I did.

Rusty, a sturdy, tall, and blond young boy was my first connection. With his mom, he had come into the speech and language clinic at Arizona State University, where I was sharpening my clinical skills to meet my college requirements and become an effective speech pathologist. I read Rusty's diagnosis in his chart: autism.

If I was going to help Rusty and his mom, it was time to ask, to learn, and to have the courage to take the first steps.

It was my father who became the next mentor in my life.

He helped me to believe that anything was possible if I obtained the knowledge (like the Scarecrow) and experience and if I wasn't afraid to ask for what I needed (like Dorothy). My father knew that someday I wanted to open up my own school for children with special needs. He used to drive me through the streets of San Francisco during my winter, spring, and summer recesses from the university, asking me if I thought certain buildings might be a good fit for the school. He helped me feel that my dreams were possible.

With my father's support, I was able to attend autism conferences and seminars. Yearly, I attended the conferences put on by the Autism society of America. I began listening and learning. I purchased a whole stack of books written by various authors, some who were professionals and others parents. I was thirsty for knowledge. I reached out to the founder of the Autism Society of America, Dr. Bernard Rimland, who later became an advisory board member on my first nonprofit school. I began reading everything I could get my hands on. I learned about Dr. Edward Ritvo and Dr. Edward Ornitz from the University of California, Los Angeles. I read about Dr. Ivar Løvaas, a psychologist who used electric shock to stop the self-abusive behaviors of children with autism residing in state hospitals.

I remember one time Dr. Rimland standing up and asking the audience how many still thought autism was an emotionally based disorder. I was surprised at the number of hands that pushed up through the air. From the very beginning of my interest in autism, I believed that it was neurologically based.

I was now on the alert to find children with autism and similar challenges and observe them. I remember the day I went to observe one preschool child who was suspected of having an autism-based learning challenge. Ten preschoolers were sitting in a group with their teacher, who was leading some type of social activity. Michael didn't join the group but stood staring at the doorknob. I wasn't sure if he wanted to open the door, close the door, or walk through the door. I remember asking him if he needed any help. He said, "Looking at circles within circles."Autism was very new to me then, and I remember thinking, "How can this little guy be so focused on those carved, circular lines in the doorknob and not want to join his excited classmates in singing, talking, moving, or playing?"

It was those simple observations that helped me gain the knowledge to understand how the sensory system in the child with autism is different from that of the typical child.

One afternoon a week, I volunteered at a "center," or what might be labeled an institution today. Children from soon after birth through their teens were placed at the center. I remember seeing one toddler with a very large head (hydrocephalus). She had soft, pink chubby arms. Her eyes fixed on mine, seeming to cry out. Her little smile was infectious. I wondered if she lay in that crib all day long. I wondered where her parents were. So, I just talked to her, touched her, and interacted with her as though she could understand everything I said. I am not sure what that might have been. I do know she smiled the entire time I spent with her, believing she could understand me. She helped me believe we should always talk to children with special needs as if they do understand and modify our talk as we learn from them. To this day, I approach students at my school with humor and high expectations at their age level.

In 1972, I graduated with my bachelor's degree and master's degree in speech pathology and audiology. I later submitted *Reach Me Teach Me*, my first book on autism, published by Academic Therapy, as my master's project. *Reach Me Teach Me* described the educational needs of children with autism and my vision of the steps in setting up the first public school program for autism, which later became my third career position on the road to autism. I was gaining knowledge as my father (my Wizard of Oz) recommended before establishing this first public school program for autism in Sacramento and later at my very own private residential and educational school.

My first position out of college was a typical speech therapist in the public schools. My one year with Hayward Unified School District couldn't end fast enough. I gravitated to all classrooms for children with special needs, wanting to help teachers learn how to help their students rather than working on stuttering, English as a second language, or articulation challenges of typical children in the district.

The Morgan Autism Center for children was my second stop along my Yellow Brick Road.

I was the speech therapist for the entire school, working with twenty students, all of whom were on the autism spectrum with a variety of communication challenges. Two years into this position, it became apparent to me that my philosophy of engaging these children and their families was very different from that of the director.

7

During my time at the Morgan Autism Center, I also met a man who believed in the journey I was on. I soon gave notice to the director at the Morgan Center and moved from the San Francisco Bay Area to the Sacramento area.

I was married, spent two very quick honeymoon days in Carmel, and reported directly for work at my new job the day after Labor Day. To my benefit, the students did not show up for school that day or the next as transportation had not been arranged. That delay allowed me time to understand why I had no materials, no furniture, and no instructional aide to support me. It provided time for me to scrounge around in book rooms and a furniture warehouse, connect with the human resource department about my aide, meet the speech therapist assigned to my classroom, and identify potential spaces, activities, and equipment the elementary school site could offer.

In 1975, there was a major change in the rights of children with disabilities. Before that time, children with any disability did not have the right to a free and appropriate public school experience. Children with autism were educated in the private sector. Now, all schools were mandated to open up classrooms for children with autism.

This is how I came to Clayton B. Wire Elementary School in Sacramento, where I opened up the first public school program for autism and met the Browns as well as Mary and Kevin, children who had spent time living at Napa State Hospital. My book *Reach Me Teach Me* was then published, and my first classroom at C. B. Wire was the test ground for my master's project.

In hindsight, I didn't really have a great deal of hands-on experience until two years after graduating from the university, when I became the speech therapist for the Morgan Center. Nevertheless, I was filled with visions and ideas about what parents were doing to get through their day and night, what researchers thought was causing the unique learning of children with autism, what some private centers had tried, and what I had learned about the communication challenges of children with special needs through my studies at Arizona State University.

Come to think about it, my quest for knowledge has never stopped. I have always continued to attend conferences, seminars, and workshops.

I continue to read articles and novels and research papers. I set up a lecture series to bring in the latest researchers, educators, therapists, and those on the spectrum to share the most recent information on autism. I continue to visit programs throughout the United States and globally.

With each new experience, new child, new family, my knowledge grew. My thirst, curiosity, and passion for knowing "How come why?" (the first words I spoke as a child) continued to expand as I looked to find ways to make a difference in the lives of those living on the autism spectrum and their families.

A Free and Appropriate Public Education

IT ALL BEGAN WITH A unique interview that included the parents of a young man with autism who would become part of the first public school classroom in the district. I had no idea what to expect from the parents that day. But I will never forget the words uttered by Mr. and Mrs. Brown during that interview. The Browns, parents of Kevin, another child with autism who had spent time at Napa State Hospital, had been told to put their son away, as they would be lucky if he turned out to be "marginally human."

My first students offered a wide variety of experiences for me. Kevin was nearly eighteen, Mary around twelve, and Tracy ten. A beautiful African-American boy, Gerald, whose smile and routine of entering the classroom through one door but leaving through another have stayed in my memory even today. Gerald was a sweet, nonverbal student whose eyes were always focused on his environment and people, trying to connect meaning to what was happening to him. His shoulders were always up around his neck. Thinking back, I realize how stressed he was each day. Finally, there was Joey: five years old, entering class each day with his three middle fingers in his mouth, bangs in his eyes, and looking as if his mom woke him up much too early for his liking.

No one at the school had ever experienced children with autism, let alone ones who had spent years in a state hospital. I made a point to connect to everyone, especially the maintenance staff on-site. They became my best friends, always helping me find useful items at the school. I strategically made friends with the teachers in the upper grades and offered to come into their classrooms in the afternoons, as my students left earlier than theirs. I offered to talk about autism and teach sign language. My motives were 1) to recruit typical children to become buddies and to look out for my students at recess time and 2) to establish a

11

community of acceptance and integration.

I will never forget my first Back to School Night at Clayton B. Wire Elementary. Not only did all my families attend, but the families of fifth- and sixth-grade students who had become buddies with my students also stopped in. They offered their thanks for getting their son or daughter involved in helping others and in understanding that each of us is different but not to be feared.

Once a month I held a parent meeting with my students' parents. I had the peer buddies to help watch my students and my instructional assistant to supervise, so parents could participate without anxiety. These gatherings built community and dispelled feelings of being isolated for my families. They also served to build a strong voice in the district to help me obtain all the supports and services I needed for my students.

One summer, the district informed me that no extended school services would be offered to my students as funding was being reduced. It was hard for me to imagine that these severely involved students would not be provided with the educational supports they required. My parents tried to convince the district that this was unfair to their children, but minds could not be changed.

So, in spite of what the district said, I embarked on setting up a summer program for my students. I found space at the local Jewish temple, I found another teacher who would join me in my effort, and I found some sponsorship dollars to cover materials, insurance, and salaries. Staff from the local newspaper, the *Sacramento Bee*, found out about the project and asked if they could run a story. I agreed. They came out, shot some great footage, the rest is history.

I received a call from the director of Special Education at Sacramento City Schools, inviting me to return to the local school site and continue the program ASAP. I clicked my heels three times and set up the summer program back in my own classroom.

During my time at C. B. Wire, I had the pleasure of welcoming two amazing senior citizens to my classrooms. They were part of a special program called the Foster Grandparent Program. Neither had ever engaged with children with autism, but both were naturals at providing heart. Both were willing to learn and had the courage to try. Grandpa

12

Banks was always calm and sturdy. He had a centering way about him. Grandma Mary was from England and her accent lightened up the room. They wiped noses, washed hands, kept a close eye on the students at recess ensuring their safety. Both were supportive of me during my nine months of pregnancy, reminding me that perhaps it was time to stop climbing the knotted ropes to model PE activities for my students.

My first son was born during my teaching experience at C. B. Wire Elementary. This meant I would be taking a maternity leave. During that time, I received a call from Mary's mom. Mary had stopped eating. It appeared that the change of teachers had created some deep anxiety for Mary. So, I contacted the teacher and we discussed my coming in to assure Mary that I was okay and still part of her community. I also made time to visit Mary at home.

How often we forget that many children with autism do not understand why people appear and then leave them. Today, using a special strategy called Social Stories, we can provide these children with a visual idea of someone leaving through pictures and words. The story and the pictures show why people are leaving, where they are going, and how children might stay in contact with them. Children can look the story over and over again, which assures them that they have not been abandoned and that someone has not just vanished into thin air, leaving them concerned and wondering.

When I returned from maternity leave, it was time to help the district set up the next two levels of the autism program: a junior high program and a high school program. I met with the junior high teacher and helped her establish her program. I agreed to set up the high school program as well and become its teacher for the next school year.

Like many programs for children with special needs, my classroom was positioned at the very back of the school campus in a rather dark portable building. When you walked up the ramp or into the classroom, you could feel the footsteps as the building was thinly built. There was one window, which I used to observe the outside life of the school.

This time my students varied in their diagnosis, but many were students on the spectrum. This time I had desks and an instructional aide before the first day of school. This time I met ahead of time with the high school counselor to find out how to build a buddy system with typical high school students.

I met with lots of resistance from regular classroom teachers in regard to mainstreaming, but once again with persistence and courage I was able to set up some integration options in math classes for my capable students. I was also able to get time in the home economics room to help my students learn to cook, and I set up a volunteer opportunity in the cafeteria for them to learn to work.

James was one of my favorite students at the high school site. For some reason, James seemed to need to put on a show for others to cover up his limitations. He was going be that "tough dude." Later I discovered that bullying had been a part of his prior school experience. James was one of my students who had learned to access the cafeteria for lunch and then return to our portable in the back. On this particular Friday, James entered the classroom after lunch and stood at the window looking out. I received a call at the same time from one of the lunch monitors saying that James had a knife and that this large, burly monitor on the phone had been unable to retrieve it from him.

Without much thought, I approached James, who was several inches taller and several pounds heavier than I, held out my hand, and asked him to give me the knife. I explained that the rule was no knives at school and that I didn't want him to get into any further trouble. I let him know that I was happy he hadn't hurt himself or anyone else and that I knew he wasn't capable of hurting anyone. My heart was beating very loud. In hindsight, I must have had a bit of courage but never realized it until then. Without a second thought, James handed me the knife.

A final incident helped me realize it was time to leave public school teaching and create the school my father told me was in my future, provided that I obtained the necessary experience and knowledge.

David was sixteen years old and nonverbal. He had many gestures that helped convey his needs, wants, and desires. He shook his head yes and no to request and deny. He used his hands to gesture toward things he wished to obtain. He made some noises to indicate his anxieties.

14

David loved to stand at the classroom window and watch the cloud formations. He used some of his noises to express his excitement as clouds took on different shapes moving across the sky. He often gestured for me to come look at this amazing phenomenon.

We were helping David learn to complete his bathroom activities independently. For months, one of my staff had helped him access the bathroom, just twenty feet away, to complete all his hygiene steps. Then for another month the staff waited outside, complimenting David on all the steps he had completed on his own. Finally, one day when David signed toilet, we let him go on his own.

We kept a lookout from our single window, ready to celebrate David's huge accomplishment. Then it happened. The incident that changed my path forever. David didn't return in a timely manner. We had watched him go in, but he had not yet come out. Had something happened during this short time?

I left the classroom and headed to the bathroom. I stood outside and called for David to come out, wanting to protect his privacy at first. No response. I raised my voice one more time and something inside me said I shouldn't wait a minute longer. I entered, and no one was in the bathroom except David. He was standing over by the sinks, shaking, and his mouth was wide open with blood in his drool. His right eyebrow had a bleeding cut on it.

My stomach was clenched, my heart pounding. I was so angry, but that is not what David needed at that moment. I moved closer to David and carefully let him know he was safe now. I ran the warm water and gently cleaned off his cuts. I asked him if he was ready to go back to class and sit down. He shook his head yes. We walked back together. I took out the first-aid kit and applied antibiotic cream. David did not want any further touching.

I had to call David's mother, Hope. I explained what had occurred. Hope said, "Karen, that's okay. Those things happen." I couldn't believe her words. I let her know that it wasn't okay. I let her know that I could no longer stand by and see this type of disrespect for others happen on my watch.

I completed an incident report and followed all the district's processes. Nothing ever happened to bring David's assaulters to accept accountability for their actions. David was nonverbal. He couldn't tell us who did this awful thing. He couldn't point out his assaulters.

I knew then that there had to be another choice for our students, that learning on a mainstream site was not the answer for all children with autism. I knew it was time to found the Kaplan Foundation.

No Longer Just a Dream

FROM THE TIME MY FATHER drove me through the streets of San Francisco, allowing me to imagine that building a school was possible, I had no doubt that someday it would actually happen.

As the Wizard of Oz told the Scarecrow, the Tin Man, and the Cowardly Lion, they had always had it inside themselves to acquire what they wanted: brains, heart, courage. My father, my Wizard of Oz, knew that I, too, had always had inside me the strength to pursue my dreams but also knew I had to first build knowledge and experiences, deepen my heart's commitment, and strengthen my courage.

Implementing the elementary program at C. B. Wire, developing the summer program for children denied a program, helping to start the junior high program for the district, and creating the high school site for students with autism enriched my experiences and broadened my knowledge. Attending conferences, reading everything I could get my hands on, and visiting programs increased my knowledge as well. Developing strong relationships with families and their sons and daughters deepened my heart's commitment.

Finishing the books *Move Ahead with Possibility Thinking* and *Tough Times Never Last But Tough People Do!*, by Robert Schuller, sealed the deal. I knew that anything was possible if I believed in the cause and never gave up trying to find the answers. I imagined possible ways to achieve my desired outcomes, believing that even if many small steps had to be created to reach the goal, I would make it happen. I wasn't afraid to ask for help, either. My dad had advised me, "If you want something bad enough, you have to be able to risk asking for it."

Looking back, I was also very lucky to be married to a man who believed I could do it. He was willing to join me on the Yellow Brick Road and support my vision for a while. That was important to the actualization of my dream.

On my path, I researched and identified ways to work with the State Department of Education, State Department of Developmental Services, and the California Regional Center System. All these agencies required stacks of documentation to certify or license a residential school for children with autism. Today sixty-five-plus objectives must be met in order to receive a certification from the State Department of Education alone.

There was also the process of forming a board of directors and a nonprofit to qualify for referrals, funding, and donations and to contract with the public school systems. I had to obtain all kinds of liability and workers' compensation insurance as well as open bank accounts and work with a payroll agency. At that time, I was a therapist and educator, not a businesswoman.

But before I could apply to any of those agencies, I had to have a school site and some way of financing all the foundational pieces (buildings, equipment, materials, curriculum, furniture, etc.) to build an entire school and home for these students. And how would I pay the salaries of the faculty I needed to hire?

So, like my father, my husband took me once again on a drive to find a site for the school. The lucky part of it all was that my husband was a real-estate agent. We agreed that we would sell our current home and purchase two houses farther up north, one in Placerville and one in Apple Hill country. We agreed that I would keep my full-time job and he his, until we secured a site and got it certified and staffed. We agreed that he would assist with the business tasks that were not yet in my realm of experience.

My dad provided the financial support to cover the costs of personnel until the billing process for services was well in place to cover those costs. You see, we would have to provide services for thirty days, then bill, and if we were lucky, funds would catch up with us forty-five to sixty days later. We were lucky.

All my aunts and uncles scrounged through their homes and came up with beds, linens, towels, dressers, kitchen appliances, and all other kinds of household necessities.

I spent hours and hours completing documents and writing a private school curriculum for children with autism to submit to the State Department of Education. Luckily, I had already written and published *Reach Me Teach Me*, my public school program guide for setting up a program for children with autism in the public sector, so I had some strong foundational information already compiled. Academic Therapy had published the book and sent it to university libraries throughout California, giving me credibility.

I met with all the state agencies, and despite all the bureaucratic red tape, the complex processes, and twisty roads ahead, I kept focused on the possibilities, just as Robert Schuller always did when building the Crystal Cathedral. I was obtaining the knowledge. I certainly had the heart and I knew I had the courage.

I was fortunate to hire some amazing faculty who were open to gaining knowledge, led with their hearts, and had the courage to try what they did not fully know. All had worked in the special needs community in some way but never received a great deal of training on autism.

We were residentially licensed as a level 4-H program by the State Department of Developmental Services and certified by the State Department of Education to support students who were on the severe range but ambulatory. Research stated that the ratio of boys to girls in the population of autism was 1 girl to 4 or 5 boys. The Kaplan Foundation, as we called the school, honoring the support of my father, reflected a very different ratio. We opened our doors with five girls and one boy. Unheard of! Mary, Beth, Leslie, Lisa A, and Lisa D attended with Kyle, our only male student and only five years old .

Mary and Beth came from the San Francisco South Bay Area. Leslie came from Lake Tahoe, Lisa D and Kyle came from Reno, Nevada, and Lisa A came from the East Bay Area. All of them were nonverbal. Four of them came in diapers. One had never slept alone in his own bed but always lay next to his mother. All had attended public school programs and were making no progress. All had extremely involved parents wanting to understand their children and see them become as independent as possible. Mary's parents were divorced, Kyle's mom was a single parent raising her son. The parents of Leslie, Beth, Lisa A, and Lisa D were still married but desperate for help.

I remember the day when all six families drove to Placerville to place their son or their daughter in the care of a young, professional woman who was passionate about making a difference, but who had never been responsible for the care of someone else's child, especially a child with a complex learning challenge like autism. That woman was me. I can only imagine the stress and anxiety they were feeling. Guilt feelings for placing a child out of his or her home, I later found out from Kyle's mom, were deep-seated in these families.

I remember that night and the next thirty nights as I slept on the couch in the front room of the home to ensure that all my team felt comfortable with these unique individuals, and that these precious lives would be well supervised and supported. For the next twenty years, I made it my mission to show up unannounced at any time of the day or night, on any day of the week or weekend, to ensure that these children were safe in the care of others employed at the Kaplan Foundation.

That first night was the most intense for me. Kyle had never slept alone, and after he had completed his nighttime routine of bathing and changing into his onesie with feet, I helped him into his twin bed. I observed as his anxiety rose and his arms began to circle faster and faster around his ears, and his body lurched forward and back. His rising scream reverberated through my body and made me feel terrible. How could I support the loss of his mother's body next to him, giving him a sense of security?

Quickly, I retrieved the rocking chair from the front living room area. Two of us took turns holding Kyle and rocking him until finally his tensed little body let go, his screams stopped, and tiredness consumed him and took him into a deep sleep. We set him in his bed, tucked him in, and hoped he'd sleep to morning.

But that night, only Mary and Beth slept through the night. Kyle, Leslie, Lisa A, and Lisa D all shuffled down the hardwood-floor hallway in their onesies into the living room where I was trying to get some sleep on the couch.

This was my true first realization of what the next twenty years might look like, as I was responsible for the lives of children on the spectrum 24/7.

I felt it was important to always have two staff on graveyard shift and to complete bed checks every fifteen minutes. A sign-in and -out sheet was posted at every bedroom door for the staff to complete so that I would feel comfortable about a child's safety when I was not on duty.

My protection had its limits, however. When Lisa was eighteen, her mom needed to accept a bed in an adult program, as spaces were extremely limited for adults with autism. Lisa would be required to leave the Kaplan Foundation as soon as she turned twenty-two anyway, so she left to be with her mother. Lisa had a well-known seizure disorder. Her seizures could occur during sleep as well and this was documented. In her adult home, they did not complete bed checks. One night, Lisa went into status epileptic and passed away. She was just nineteen.

Only after her daughter's death did Lisa's mom uncover the fact that Lisa was never checked on during the night shift. Through legal action, the family tried to hold the program accountable but received no support. Having been part of Lisa's life since she was five years old, I was heart-stricken, hearing the story of her passing.

I was also incredibly angry that the program could continue to operate, having neglected to support the needs of a special individual like Lisa.

On the Road Again

PLACERVILLE WAS A GOOD BEGINNING, but it served only six children and recruiting faculty was challenging due to its distance from a major city. My husband and I took that special ride one more time, looking for a piece of land that could support my program expansion dreams. We found the perfect site, a five-acre piece with a large ranch-style home, a barn and stables, and a fenced-in swimming pool. We were on the Yellow Brick Road once again.

We sold both homes in Placer County and purchased two homes in Orangevale, one to live in and one for Kaplan Foundation expansion. I completed all the state certification paperwork to move the school to the new site, completed all kinds of home improvements to support eight students in the home instead of six, and converted barns and stables to classrooms. We had been on the Placerville site for only a little over one year, but the new site had so much more promise.

I connected with Sacramento State University, which included teaching in its credentialing program, and began recruiting special education and psychology students to work with our students. I also reached out to the University of California, Davis, and recruited from its special needs programs. I was lucky to teach in its extension program and connect to students hungering to learn about autism.

The Kaplan Foundation home began with one home serving six students and increased to four homes within five years as we built our entire school base to twenty-five students. Additional day students were placed as well during this time.

The team grew in various ways as well, from one teacher (me) to two, three, and then four. We added a speech therapist and an art therapist. In the summer, we hired a swim instructor. We added an amazing nutritional consultant, Dr. Patricia Kane, now a leading researcher and clinician in biomedical approaches to neurological challenges (NeuroLipid

Research Foundation (www.neurolipid.org). Finally, we hired instructional aide support. The day we opened our doors on Santa Juanita Avenue in Orangevale, the children who lived at the school enjoyed a gluten-free and casein-free meal program. Remember, this was 1979! No additives, no refined sugars, fresh fruits and vegetables delivered twice a week! All part of helping these children develop healthy bodies and brains. Dr. Kane and I worked with the local pediatrician to explore candida challenges in these children and addressed those issues whenever we encountered them. Dr. Kane and I also worked with a local allergy specialist to identify and treat any allergies in our student population.

The only medications these children remained on were seizure disorder medications. Mellaril, Haldol, and Thorazine were gradually decreased by their doctors. To help support learning, we tried supplements developed by Dr. Bernard Rimland, father of a young man with autism and founder of the Autism Society of America.

I remember the day the children's dentist expressed surprise that the children's teeth were in such amazing condition. He was curious about their diet and hygiene habits. We were proud to give him the details. Our children also seemed to sleep well. Their all-around health was very good. I don't remember taking sick children to the doctor very often. They were seen yearly for their routine wellness checkups and by their neurologist to oversee their seizure medication, but not much more.

The Children of the Kaplan Foundation

THE CHILDREN WERE REQUIRED TO swim or learn to swim, bike or learn to ride a bike, and run or walk for designated amounts of time. They also enjoyed jumping on our amazing trampoline, until one day the California Department of Education no longer approved our use of it, even with huge amounts of insurance. It was such a loss to our students.

One of those students was Andrew, a young man with curly hair who was very tall for his age and very thin. Andrew finger- and arm-stimmed (a repetitive flicking and rotating of his fingers, hands, and arms) throughout his day. Today we would say he was "self-regulating," trying to stay engaged and calm by displaying repetitive motor movements. When Andrew climbed onto that trampoline and got going, jumping higher and higher into the air, his face lit up. His hands and arms, generally lifted to ear level and higher during his stimming, would come down by his side and support his heavy pushing into the mat of the trampoline. The longer he bounced, the happier he became. You see, to help his body calm down and stay regulated in his world of oversensitivity, he was getting proprioceptive input (joint compression).

The twenty-year history of the Kaplan Foundation could fill a huge hardbound book with emotional stories about the challenges and successes of the amazing children who lived, learned, and played there.

Many children, diapered when they entered, learned to take care of their needs. Students who never enjoyed typical children's activities of swimming, biking, going to parks, or roller-skating all learned to engage in them. Children who were limited in their community experiences before entering the Kaplan Foundation were accessing every park, museum, store, café, movie theater, and sports center that the Sacramento Valley had to offer.

Children who were totally taken care of by their mothers or fathers learned to dress themselves, shower, brush their teeth, do their own laundry, make their own meals, shop, and respect others' belongings as well as their environments.

As it is with life, not all our stories are filled with success or joy.

One of my saddest stories occurred with one of my Lisas. Lisa talked to me through her eyes and her dancing feet. When she was happy, her feet moved just like those penguins in the movie *Happy Feet*, and her hands flapped by her side like beautiful hummingbirds. Looking back, I wish I had known then what I do today about sensory dysregulation (the inability to understand and utilize the sensory information coming into our brain through our senses and body to move through our day). Her lips, chapped from constant licking, were a sign. Her rapid breathing and her shoulders hunched up around her ears were signs. Slapping herself, pulling her hair out, and grabbing others were all signs of sensory overload and anxiety.

Lisa made so many positive gains at the foundation, but as she entered her teens and puberty took over, her anxieties only increased. She became stronger and more unpredictable. Her dysregulated actions affected other students and staff who tried to support her. They increased to a level where the only solution left was to admit we didn't have the answer and, in order to ensure the safety of the others, to inform the family that it was time for Lisa to move to a program that could help.

But there were no programs available, and Lisa was moved to a state hospital, the last place I ever wanted to see any of my Kaplan children end up. I only remember the deep heartache I felt the day Lisa left. I felt I had failed Lisa and I had failed her family. It was at that time I remembered the Wizard of Oz asking the Tin Man, "Why do you want a heart anyway?" I wondered why at that moment also, because mine was crushed.

My heart also jumped the day I received a call from my weekend staff. Tracy G. was no longer on the property. It was nearly sundown. It appeared he had carefully taken off his shoes, set them at the front door, and left the property.

I jumped into my red Mazda and headed to the Santa Juanita House. I got there in record time without a traffic ticket, which was in itself a feat.

I had informed the staff to call the local sheriff's department, and so the sheriff was already out looking. The staff said that Tracy had been out of their sight for only five minutes. We knocked on neighbors' doors and drove down every street within a five-mile radius. My heart was in my stomach. The thought of having to call Tracy's mom was heavy on my brain. Then, the call came from the sheriff. It appeared Tracy was not exactly happy with our meal plan for that evening and decided to head to Wendy's just a few blocks away to enjoy some of the customers' orders. Tracy was a very tall young man with autism. He was nonverbal and engaged in some very intricate hand and arm movements. I am sure Tracy had given some of the customers a shake-up that night. The sheriff had been able to get Tracy to follow the officers to their car and they were on their way back to the foundation.

I met the officers back at the school. They were extremely understanding and offered their help to us anytime. I was so grateful. I still had to make that call, but at least I could tell Tracy's mom and dad that he was safe. They were understanding and grateful that night.

No one would have ever expected Tracy to sneak out, specially me. He had the Gozers (my made-up word for elopement) in public school but only to leave the classroom to sift through tanbark on the playground. Moving forward, we made sure to put burgers and French fries on our menu. We also increased our alarm system support on doors. Like the Scarecrow, we acquired new knowledge, and we did not experience the Gozers again.

Then there was Mark M., a very smart and a very interesting boy with autism. He was verbal, able to make his needs known to all. He learned quickly how to complete all activities of daily living, but he seemed to always be concerned about what might happen if he were to engage in some unacceptable behaviors. He frustrated easily when his questions were not answered. When he was upset he would move his body in odd contortions and squeeze his shoulders up around his ears and tense his face.

Dr. Kane, our pediatrician, and the foundation's allergy specialist felt something was internally going on with Mark. One day, Mark's anxiety pushed him to pick up the living room TV and throw it in my direction. In hindsight I am not sure how I did catch that TV that day. I certainly must have possessed the strength and courage of the Cowardly Lion.

With the results of the tests and Dr. Kane's wisdom in interpreting Mark's behavior, we removed casein from his diet and never saw the extremes of aggression ever again. We also made sure Mark engaged in physical exercise daily, and we provided feedback to his somewhat obsessive questions, teaching him that we were more interested in his asking questions of a positive nature.

Elizabeth's story truly shows how knowledge, heart, and courage are so important. Beth, as we called her, always moved slowly. She had a cute little pixie haircut and, as I recall, blue eyes. She was a teenager when she came to the Kaplan Foundation. She had not been making progress in her public school program, and through the help of an attorney, her parents were able to get her placed in our school. She often kept her lips tightly pursed. She often looked up toward one side. When frustrated she might hit the top of her hand or arm, tense up her face, or try to scream, but she was hard-pressed to scare anyone with the meager sounds that came out.

Beth's progress was slow: a bit too slow for her school district. After funding her for a couple of years, the district decided to tell the parents it was not willing to invest in Elizabeth's education at the Kaplan Foundation as she did not have the cognitive capacity to benefit. I can only imagine the sadness and despair her mother and father felt that day. Who were these professionals suggesting that their teen daughter did not possess the capacity to grow and learn? What crystal ball did they possess or research document did they read that supported this statement.

The family hired an amazing attorney to fight the case. Calm, organized, heartfelt, and articulate, Mike Zatopa was well educated in special education law. I had a great deal of respect for him, trusting that he would do his very best for Beth and her family. The attorney for the district had a reputation for being a real bitch, her name rhyming with witch, which was not surprising.

The case went from discussions in the attorney's offices to mediation and finally to the courtroom. I was asked to be a key witness and had to be available for cross-examination by this woman. Mike worked with me, encouraging me to voice my knowledge and, as always, lead with my heart.

The attorney tried to discredit my background, then poked fun at published articles that suggested that the Kaplan Foundation was the "Cadillac of Autism Programs." At one point in the hearing, the presiding judge stopped her questioning and warned her against shaking her finger at me.

Others were brought to the stand that day, and professionals from the district stated their opinion on the limited capacity of this young teen with autism. I watched the faces of Beth's mom and dad as their eyes saddened with each piece of information presented about the limitations of their daughter. It was horrible.

The Kaplan Foundation was the only school that saw the potential of each person who came to it. This experience only strengthened my mission to create programs that would believe in each child's abilities, not his or her disabilities. This experience also solidified even more my conviction that I would need the courage and the heart to continue gaining knowledge to help children and their families in the field of autism spectrum disorders.

The Autism Quilt,
Kaplan Remembered

I CAREFULLY TOOK DOWN THE quilt that hung behind my desk at the Kaplan Foundation, folded it several times, making it a two-foot-by-three-foot rectangle, and placed it neatly in the bottom of one of the many boxes I used to pack up the past twenty years of my life devoted to creating, developing, and implementing a residential school for children with autism. Those fifty-two squares, each eight by eight inches, told the individual stories of the fifty-two children who changed my life.

By my side was my soon-to-be best friend and mom of one of the very first children placed at the Kaplan Foundation in March of 1979. Her son's name was one of the very first to appear on that quilt. Meg had led the creation of this amazing quilt to honor my twenty years committed to finding solutions and help for children with autism. It was this mom who took the time and had the patience to connect each square together, so that in the years to come I would be reminded of the children and families I had helped along the way.

But on this night, this mom was helping me gather up the years of my work. On this night, the jealousy and the anger of one man were allowed to win over a young girl's longtime dream to create little miracles. On this night, I felt how fear and control were allowed to win over fairness and the dream of making a difference.

So, I buried that quilt with my hurt in one of those boxes and stored them and most of the intense feelings away: first in the house in the cul-de-sac in Granite Bay, California, then in the house by the lake, then in the attic of the house in San Anselmo, in Marin County, and finally in the linen closet of my Terra Linda home.

It wasn't until Saturday morning, August 15, 2009, ten years later, that I finally unfolded the quilt and laid it across the back of the green couch

31

in my office, carefully reading each square and trying to imagine, once again, the face, the voice, the unusual behaviors of the child or family who had moved my life in its apparently predestined direction on the road with autism.

I found that seeing and touching the quilt was helping me better understand one of the important journeys on my road. I found the quilt helped me to release the hurt buried inside me and also to see what I had accomplished. I thought that perhaps one day I might write a book entitled *The Autism Quilt* and share some stories about those amazing children and families in hopes it might comfort them. Perhaps one or more of those fifty-two squares, each eight by eight inches, might help me share how a child with autism affected my life's journey and provide some useful ideas on how to support someone living each day on the spectrum.

One of my first reactions to seeing the quilt and touching the names on each square was to realize that my ex had never really taken any of the important things away from me. He had never taken away my passion, the knowledge I had acquired, and he had never taken away the experiences that brought me courage to continue on the road or the memories and successes I lived.

Next, with a smile on my face, I visualized the uniqueness of each child's little behaviors. For Sarah, who had come directly out of the state hospital, it was how she walked backward and made sure to lick each object on her way. For Mary it was her head down, arms swirling, and her fingers flicking the air as she made a kind of whistling sound. For Mark it was throwing a TV nearly across the family room or wondering what would happen if you hit someone over the head with a baseball bat. For Kyle it was gagging on watermelon or seeing how the palm of his adolescent hand fit over the face of a baby. For Lisa it was climbing on the very top of the playground bars, her hands flapping vigorously above her head. For Tina it was holding the tiniest piece of lint between her thumb and pointer finger. And for Michael it was reading the *Wall Street Journal*, the letters on everyone's T-shirts, and the manufacturer emblems on every car that passed.

Talking only in a whisper, that was Scott. Sneaking out to Wendy's, his shoes in his hands, that was Tracy. Disrobing, running around the swimming pool as he dangled the yellow shoe laces in front of his face, that was Christopher. Asking permission not to look into your eyes while trying to understand what you were saying, that was Max. Happy feet dancing, that was my Lisa.

Then I remembered the different ways those children communicated their feelings, needs, and dislikes by crying, screaming, biting themselves, pulling their hair, laughing, kicking, leading me by my hand, sitting next to me, falling out of their chair, pacing, jumping, bolting, clapping their hands at the side of their ear, loud sounds, soft sounds, short sounds and long sounds, echoing what I last said, repeating phrases, spelling, and, of course, singing.

I was reminded that each child on the quilt was admitted to the Kaplan Foundation because I saw hope for him or her. I believed each could learn. I believed if the families became part of the multidisciplinary team, anything was possible.

Max was a tall, blond, and lanky teenager, with horned-rimmed glasses that he pushed up onto his nose many times a day. He had an awkward gait. Max was diagnosed with high-functioning autism or perhaps what is known today as Asperger. Max taught me a few great lessons on my road.

On his quilted square, "Max" was written in black glued letters above a sitting Winnie the Pooh. The words "Oh, Bother" were lightly written next to Winnie the Pooh's head. Letters of the alphabet in primary colors and balloons floated nearby. The date, "September 28, 1983," was written at the bottom of the square.

Max was the highest cognitive student placed at the Kaplan Foundation in the twenty years of my directorship. He read, wrote, understood mathematics, and engaged in conversation with me.

I do not remember exactly what brought Max into my office that fall day, but I will always remember the wonderful insight he gave me. His simple request helped me begin to appreciate the sensory challenges he and other children faced. Max asked if he could glance at me for just a moment and then complete his request without continuing to make eye contact. "It's hard for me to look at your eyes, Karen, and hear what you are saying to me and answer you back all at the same time." Wow!!

I remember our agreeing that he would connect with my face upon entering my office or at the beginning of a conversation, but that it would be okay for him to look down or away the rest of the time.

In the early years of behavior intervention it was a standard procedure to expect and ensure that a child makes sustained eye contact. It was, in fact, the social norm. Children like Max were reinforced with every kind of edible and every kind of social reinforcement possible to increase the likelihood that they would make prolonged eye contact. It was standard to see this behavior goal written on every child with autism's IEP (individual education plan).

Now students view films and act out plays and skits to understand how to position their bodies to indicate an openness to conversation or to understand when someone is bored with a topic, in a hurry, tired, or angry and frustrated.

Our professionals and our families now have the work of Michelle Garcia Winner, Jed Baker, Brenda Myles, and Dr. Janette McAfee, to name just a few, to help teach social thinking and our students navigate the social world.

What I did know then was how important it was for me to create activities for Max and other students to engage in, together and within the community to increase the likelihood that they would be able to socially interact in their home schools, in their own homes, and in their local communities.

Max helped prepare meals and participated in all the meals, which were family-style at the Kaplan Foundation. On special occasions, the linens were even brought out and flowers or holiday decorations placed in the center of the table.

Max and others prepared meals with the staff through verbal cueing, visual pictures, gestures, or actual hand-over-hand support. In the kitchen, they stirred, whipped, spread, or blended items before cooking. They set and cleared off the tables with a meal buddy.

They all learned to wash and cut vegetables for salads and locate, obtain, and add ingredients to dishes. Using a toaster, operating a microwave, using a can opener—manual and electric—were all parts of learning to participate with others in a home environment and ways to improve the fine-motor, motor-planning, and sequencing skills they would need to be functioning adults.

At the table, staff joined Max and his housemates, modeling appropriate table manners and eating habits and conversational speech. They facilitated requests like "Please pass the salt" and modeled comments and questions like "What did you do at school today?"

Daily recreational activities were planned, and our students enjoyed going to local libraries, amusement parks, regional parks, and bowling alleys. They went on outings to Christmas tree farms and pumpkin patches, and the teens engaged in trips to the mall, where they learned how to "cruise" and window-shop. They also learned to drink hot chocolate at local cafés, see movies, attend sports events, see a play, or listen to a concert at theaters.

Staff supported students in those activities by demonstrating and modeling appropriate behaviors, physically prompting engagement, and facilitating communication scripts.

Max and others learned to share space, to take turns, to wait for their needs to be met, and to work in a group. There were always two to a bedroom.

Faculty was always paired with one or more students, and there was an expectation that students would always learn with another child by their side.

Lunch was a community event, art and music classes were held in groups of four to six, and often physical education activities (swimming, jogging) were done in small groups.

Students joined birthday celebrations, went on picnics with staff and parents, and learned to participate in Special Olympics.

Novelty was always hard for Max. He and others resisted new activities and became overwhelmed in the beginning. But with the right kind of support, structuring, patience, and pre-teaching, Max and every other student succeeded in group activities.

As I looked once again at Max's square on the quilt, I realized he had found the courage to ask for what he needed in order to connect and learn. He then opened my eyes to search for different solutions, ideas, and knowledge to help children with ASD (autism spectrum disorder) acquire social thinking and social interaction skills. Finally, Max helped me realize how I always need to consider the feelings of each individual living each day on the spectrum, and to understand how they might see and feel the world. Max helped me be in touch with my heart.

Kyle's eight-by-eight-inch square had his named spelled out in orange glue. A piece of soft yellow fleece was in the background. Under the two cutout PJ feet bottoms his mom had glued in the center of the square was written, "Thank you for caring about me." Those PJ feet bottoms were the ones that rubbed against the hardwood floors each time Kyle woke up in the middle of the night, unable to sleep, and wandered into the family room where I slept during the first thirty days at the Kaplan Foundation.

How many sleepless nights could these children's moms and dads endure before their families would fall apart from their inability to work, take care of siblings, or maintain a healthy relationship with their partners? How long could they go without clarity of thought? How long could they continue to be present in their lives feeling physically exhausted?

So, it had been up to me to design a program that would help those PJ bottoms stay in their bed and sleep and help their moms deal with the guilt that they felt each time a neighbor, a friend, or a family member looked at them accusingly for placing their child in a residential program.

Kyle's program involved integrating many components: diet, toilet training, structure, physical exercise, speech therapy, and learning skills of daily living and community access. It involved engaging his mom so she could understand how we were teaching Kyle and follow through at home.

Kyle did not use words to communicate, but those who took the time to develop a relationship with Kyle knew when he was happy, frustrated, or upset. When he stood on his tiptoes and moaned, or rotated both his hands and arms in circles by the side of his body, they knew by the intensity of his moans and the furrowing of his brow whether he was excited or frustrated. When his eyes squinted, his nose turned up, and he laughed, they knew that he was happy. When his head rotated and his face turned red, they knew that he was anxious.

But for those who did not know Kyle's communication system and wanted to communicate with him, that was not good enough. That was not good enough when he needed to let someone know he had to use the bathroom, when he was hungry, or when he was thirsty. That was not good enough when he wanted to ride a bike or go for a swim and not good enough when he needed to let someone know he was tired.

The first communication strategy we tried with Kyle was called Total Communication: signing and talking simultaneously. Staff were trained on how to sign basic nouns and verbs when they spoke, and his family was given a small sign language book with the basic signs that Kyle was learning. A list of the ten to twenty most common requests that Kyle made throughout the day was created, and those were the first signs he was taught to use (requests for eat, drink, sleep, use the bathroom). The pronoun "I" and the verb "want" were added, but Kyle often left them off unless he was prompted to use a whole sentence. He exaggerated the sign "want" by moving his hands and arms toward himself instead of using just the palms of his hands.

Kyle's language therapy involved demonstrating his understanding by pointing to pictures, giving a picture of a desired object to a teacher, and following first one-part and then two-part directions. His entire day was filled with language experiences: picking out the correct pieces of clothing each day to wear, requesting something to eat or drink at breakfast, lunch, or dinner, demonstrating his understanding of "on," "under," and "next to" by following the teacher's directions, setting the table, or unloading the dishwasher. He learned verbs by engaging in the action as staff labeled his activity and later asked him to sign or select a picture of the activity he had engaged in (skating, sweeping, vacuuming, mopping, running, swimming, climbing, swinging, or pouring). He practiced one-on-one with a speech therapist, in a group with the teacher, and then with the residential staff during the home program.

His dresser drawers had pictures on the outside showing the items located in the drawers (socks, underwear, T-shirts), so he learned to match and locate his clothing quickly. While doing the laundry, he learned to match socks after taking them out of the dryer and to fold them before putting them away in his drawers. While unloading forks, knives, and spoons from the dishwasher, he learned to sort them in the utensil drawers and to stack plates and bowls in the appropriate section on the cupboard shelves.

Kyle learned to make his bed, brush his teeth, wash his hands, shower, set a table, make a salad, load a dishwasher and a washing machine, dress himself, and many other skills of daily life through a procedure called Backward Chaining, a behavior-modification strategy where each task was broken down into many individual steps needing to be completed to finish the objective. Then with prompting (help), whether visual, verbal, or physical, Kyle learned the entire task (last step first) and could complete it without any prompting (help).

We demonstrated, and then Kyle imitated, or we physically moved Kyle through the steps, then finally verbally dialogued with Kyle through the task until he could do it without any modeling or verbalizing. Today, I would have used the Mayer-Johnson picture icon program for each step of a task and Kyle would have followed the pictorial sequence, learning to complete the task. Kyle could have also learned how to complete the task through Video Modeling. Research has shown us that children like Kyle are able to view a video of an activity being done and then complete that task more successfully.

Exercise was an integral part of Kyle's program. Every morning before school, all the students walked or jogged around our homemade track to get calm before starting their school day and to prepare for Special Olympics. Next, all students spent time daily on the full-size trampoline. For Kyle, jumping seemed to decrease his self-stimulating behaviors, as it did for other students at the foundation. The longer they bounced on the trampoline, engaging in deep knee bending and seat-to-feet actions, the more we could count on a reduction of their self-stimulating actions.

Rollerblading was another favorite of Kyle's, and how he loved to crash directly into the wooden fence, feeling the deep pressure of the wood beating against his skates. He learned to ride a bike and, wouldn't you know it, he also loved to push that bike against the wooden fence and feel the impact.

Kyle loved the water. He loved swimming underwater where his body could be totally surrounded by the deep pressure the water offered him. His mom used to put a life jacket on him, tie a 100-foot rope to the back of the jacket, and let him swim for hours in the lake where his family enjoyed camping.

Today, through the research of licensed occupational therapist Dr. Jane Ayers, we understand how proprioceptive activities (jumping, pushing, pulling, climbing, swimming, and heavy lifting) help children with autism regulate themselves and reduce their own anxieties. Sensory integration intervention and sensory processing intervention play a key role in the therapeutic planning for children with autism. Today we know through research at the MIND Institute (UC Davis Medical Investigation of Neurodevelopmental Disorders) that proprioceptive learning is the most beneficial way to help a child with autism under-stand how to do things.

When I reflect on Kyle's eight-by-eight-inch square and remember his story, I am reminded of his mother's courage to place him in my care, his mother's loving heart, and her commitment to finding help for her son. I think of the knowledge I was able to acquire, finding ways to help him. I am reminded how important it is to never ever give up on our Yellow Brick Roads. I am reminded that there will be tornadoes, and wickedness, and objects thrown at us along the way, but that these are only temporary obstacles. They will pass, and we will find another way to the Emerald City, over the rainbow, or back to Kansas.

Marni's Square

THE CAPITAL LETTERS M-A-R-N-I WERE written in bright pink on Marni's eight-by-eight-inch square. A cutout of Minnie Mouse with her bright red bow, loaded with hearts, was pasted onto a pink-and-blue cloth background. A pink "1991" was written on the right-hand side of the square.

Marni liked to practice writing her name, numbers, and upper- and lower-case letters. She could count. She seemed to understand quantity and she liked to color.

Her assessments had shown that her developmental profile went from one year, eleven months, to eight years, five months, depending on the skill area evaluated. She exhibited some behaviors that concerned her parents, such as kicking, hitting, and biting others. She screamed and head-banged on the floor. At times she picked at sores, played with her food, ate nonedibles, and sifted leaves.

Providing structure and consistency helped Marni. Making sure she ate healthy food, was engaged in sensory activities and speech therapy, and was learning to make choices helped decrease her challenging behaviors. We also broke down all daily living tasks into meaningful steps that reduced anxiety and increased understanding and learning.

Marni learned easily to wash her hands, dry herself, make breakfast, load the dishwasher, set and clear the table, dress, put her clothes away, and twenty-five other skills of daily living.

In school, she was learning to raise her hand, sign and say her needs, point, operate a computer, use scissors, participate in her music group, order at an ice cream store, make a purchase at a clothing store, and greet others.

One night in November, Marni gave us the scare of our lives. She decided to take advantage of everyone's preoccupation with one of her housemates. Marni had gone to her room to get her shoes, or so the team thought. Kerry was helping Alana tie her shoes, Vanessa was assisting Anna in the bathroom, Rachel was helping Nicole put on her sweatshirt, and a trainee was next to Kerry, learning how to help Alana. At 5:06 p.m. a head count occurred in the entryway to the house before everyone was to take a quick walk before dinner. Marni did not line up. The staff looked for her, but she was nowhere in the house or backyard. The staff realized that someone from the earlier shift had forgotten to reset the house alarm, which would have alerted them to Marni's current elopement. Two of the staff got into the van to search the neighborhood. The team left a message for me, contacted the sheriff's department, and just prayed she would be found. At 5:45 p.m. an officer called to let us know they had picked up Marni. She had walked into a neighbor's home, and the family called the sheriff.

The staff finally stopped holding their breath that night. They met and discussed the errors in supervision and the necessity of maintaining the 2-to-1 ratios at all times. The a.m. shift and p.m. shift supervisors met to ensure that the alarm system was always in place. Everyone felt badly.

You may wonder how I can remember all the details of that one day so long ago, but it was required that every special incident be documented and then sent to the family. There in the piles of documents Marni's mom had sent me, in the gray storage container, was the incident report. I can't help but remember how awful it was to have to call parents and to tell them that their son or daughter wasn't safe. I felt I had let them down. All the policies, all the procedures in the world, and all the meetings held to discuss what went wrong and what we could do better never seemed to be foolproof. Mistakes would be made, and I was grateful that nothing truly terrible ever happened to a child in the twenty years I had led the foundation.

Lisa's Square

It was a piece of soft, pink cloth, eight inches by eight inches, with one white sock glued on it and Lisa's name written on the side. Lisa would take her white socks off and twirl one of them in front of her face, mouth as well wide open, marveling at the pattern the sock made as she twirled it around with her wrist and forearm.

Lisa was one of the very first little ones entrusted to my care. She had thick, soft red hair and this mesmerizing smile. When she was excited, she would shake her head, not up and down but from side to side, mouth wide open, making a sound like "youie, youie," arms stretched out in front of her, hands rotating left and right like she was turning the knobs on the stereo. If she was sitting, she would lift her legs out in front of her, and her feet and legs would mirror her outstretched arms and hands, joining in rotating movements.

Lisa sucked her thumb to soothe herself and isolated herself when upset. I remember one day I was in my office writing a report when Lisa ran out of her bedroom at the back of the house, crying and upset. Any attempt to offer comfort was met by her holding her hand up, keeping space between us, and moving farther away. I gave her space. She turned her back to me and, staring out the large picture window in my office, paced back and forth head down, twirling her sock, her crying lessening.

I watched her reflection in the window as she calmed herself down and was then ready to return to her daily routine, the sock now quiet by her side or resting on the floor nearby.

Lisa was nonverbal, not toilet trained, and unable to sustain engagement in any activity for more than a few seconds. She loved to get herself high up, whether on the very top of the playground equipment at the school in Orangevale, or up on the window ledge of her bedroom window in our first school in Placerville.

I remember how Lisa's dad spoke about her. I loved watching the way he adored this little redheaded child with autism who could not say "Daddy" or let him know how safe he made her feel. You could see that love in his eyes as he sat still and waited for her to sit next to him. And I loved the way Ken accepted his daughter for who she was and always maintained a sense of hope.

In the late '80s, it was thought that about 40 percent of children with autism would acquire a seizure disorder. During adolescence, Lisa had her first seizure. Doctors asked us to maintain a log and keep a close eye on her. Within six months from the first seizure, Lisa started to have seizures on a regular basis, and her family worked with a doctor who placed Lisa on medication. We continued to supervise Lisa, especially during the evenings when seizures happened more frequently during sleep. We completed bed checks every fifteen minutes at the Kaplan Foundation, noting a child's activity level on the bed check form.

When learning her skills of daily living, Lisa responded well to structure, visual supports, and task analysis (a system of breaking each task into its steps). She often required physical support, which then faded to tactile, verbal, and finally visual. She learned best one-on-one but learned to work with one or two others and wait her turn during school tasks. Toilet training was implemented during the first six months using a procedure that Nathan H. Azrin and Richard M. Foxx discuss in their book *Toilet Training in Less Than a Day*. Lisa reached her goal one year later.

Lisa had a set routine each day, which helped her understand what would happen first and then next. School started at 9:00 a.m., so she was awakened between 7:30 and 8:00 a.m., then supported in making her bed, picking out her clothes for the day, placing her PJs in the hamper, getting dressed, and enjoying breakfast.

She set her own place at the breakfast table by matching an outlined placemat with the glass, plate or bowl, napkin, and utensils on it. She obtained all the items she needed for the meal and prepared as much of her breakfast as possible. She was required to clear her table and load the dishwasher, which completed the meal process. Then, she brushed her teeth, combed her hair, gathered her backpack for school, and walked to the back of the property where the classrooms were located.

In between the house and the school were the swimming pool, the playground, and a grassy area for picnicking, Frisbee, and kickball. Along one side of the classrooms was the track area where Lisa and her classmates walked or jogged before school, frequently throughout the day, and again in the afternoon. On the other side of the classrooms were the basketball court and trampoline.

Lisa wasn't the least bit interested in playing basketball, but she loved jumping as high as she could on the trampoline and doing seat drops over and over and over again. She was also not interested in Frisbee or kickball, but she went along with all the jogging expectations and later ran in track events at Special Olympics held at Sacramento State University each year.

One of our most important goals was to identify a way to help Lisa communicate her needs and wants. Total Communication (signing and talking) was used throughout her day, and Lisa learned to use the sign for "eat" and "bathroom" consistently. Pointing and giving pictures of her communication intentions were also ways Lisa communicated her needs and wants. She followed many one-part directions, at first with physical prompting and later with visual cuing, letting us know her receptive language was higher than her expressive language.

When planning Lisa's program, I asked the teacher and her parents to ask themselves one important question before setting goals. If Lisa doesn't do it, will someone else have to? Those were the first goals set and measured. Those would be the goals that would help Lisa become independent, so those were the goals implemented and measured. Through the years Lisa required less physical support to meet them.

During after-school hours and on weekends, Lisa and her house buddies engaged in every activity their normal peers engaged in: playing at parks, bowling, going to museums, taking walks, attending festivals, making trips to the library, going to the mall, dining out, going to the zoo, having picnics at the lake, swimming, and roller-skating.

Lisa's mom picked her up on Fridays after school for monthly home visits and later for longer holiday visits. She was first asked to observe Lisa in the home program, seeing how the staff helped Lisa complete skills of daily living. Then the staff went home with Lisa for a weekend visit to help support her mom and dad as they worked with Lisa in her own home.

Lisa's parents stayed connected to her through monthly written correspondence. They spoke to the residential staff in the evenings to keep up to date on her progress in the home and community, and they spoke to the teacher to keep up on her educational process.

Lisa's mom always attended her Individual Educational Planning meetings with the placing school district and Individual Program Planning meetings with the regional center.

Lisa's mom and dad and brother came up for Special Olympics weekends, cheering Lisa on in her events.

Although the Kaplan Foundation served children educationally until age twenty-two, it often took a special waiver from the Regional Center to maintain the children in the program past their eighteenth birthday. I always received the waiver, thank goodness. But when an adult placement opportunity came up for Lisa, her parents, fearing there would not be an adult residential option later for Lisa, moved her from the Kaplan Foundation to a Bay Area adult program closer to her family. She had been at the foundation since she was six. She had been one of my original six. I would miss her smile, her red hair, her quirky sounds, and her innocence.

The years of work at the Kaplan Foundation filled my heart with volumes of memories. The children created stories I will never forget.

Andrew's Story

ANDREW'S MOM, MARY, OUTLINED HIS hands on a piece of cloth. Then she carefully cut them out and glued them on the eight-by-eight-inch royal blue quilt square. The hands were joined. Andrew's name was written on the wrist of one hand and mine on the other. The words "Into the Hands of Friends" were written on the royal blue cloth. The date "March 16, 1986" appeared on the square as well.

Several years after the Kaplan Foundation received Andrew, his family having placed him in our hands, his mom, Mary, sent me a poem she had written called "Kaplan: Our Best Friend."

> Into the hands of strangers
> We placed our boy of four
> With grieving hearts and blinding tears
> We slowly went out the door
>
> There was no comfort the long trip home
> In the fact that we had no choice
> For who should have to leave a child
> Where he could hear no familiar voice
>
> Who would love this little boy
> As only a family could
> And comfort him when he is scared
> And praise him when he is good
>
> So we prayed dear God to bring the best
> Of people to act as kin
> To hold him close and give him hugs
> And find the person within

With each passing year we watched
And he was loved it was clear to see
This child who once had no hope at all
Was becoming the best he could be

Goals were set and tasks assigned
By an exceptional caring team
Finally resulting in skills achieved
And performed with an impish gleam

God gave us all that we did ask
He gave us so much more
When we asked for the best of strangers
To care for that child of four

For in the home in which he lives
And at the school that he attends
He did not put him into the hands of strangers
But into the hands of friends

Andrew came to the Kaplan Foundation in 1986 at age four. By 1991 he had a few single words and signs to communicate what he wanted from others. The speech therapist worked a great deal on developing his ability to request foods, drinks, and activities he was interested in and to ask to use the bathroom. She also worked on expanding his ability to imitate sounds and put them together to form meaningful words.

Andrew enjoyed engaging in motor activities such as playing soccer, riding a bike, and walking. He was working on expanding his fine motor skills in order to complete writing tasks and self-help tasks.

The education staff were helping him to use utensils during snack time and lunch and providing hand-over-hand support to tie his shoes and verbal support to brush his teeth after lunch.

Prevocational tasks were presented during school hours through a special Work Skill Development Series, and he was learning a variety of assembly tasks, color-matching tasks, and sequencing tasks.

To build socialization, Andrew engaged in sharing job chores and playing indoor and outdoor games with his fellow classmates.

Andrew engaged in the community by making weekly visits to a variety of community environments such as the library, the grocery store, or restaurants. The staff facilitated social skills, motor skills, communication skills, and problem solving.

The teacher established goals by administering the Brigance Diagnostic Inventory of Early Development. This particular assessment identified areas of need in gross motor, fine motor, self-help, speech & language, general knowledge, and academic readiness.

In his home program Andrew worked on picking out his own clothing, dressing, zipping, buttoning, toileting, showering, washing his hands, brushing his teeth, setting the table, hanging up his clothes, folding, making his bed, and using his fork. Each year more goals were added on, even when many other goals were still in progress, because the more skills our students were expected to participate in, the more they grew to reach independence. We did not wait for all steps of every task to be completed. We were happy with his engagement in the activity and closer and closer approximation to reaching the goal.

Kaplan used a three-step support system to teach new skills. The idea was to give Andrew the least amount of help first (visual cue), then add verbal support if needed, and finally provide physical support of some type to teach the skill if it was still too difficult for Andrew. We used backward-chaining strategies requiring Andrew to complete the last step in the skill chain without support first.

We had hoped that Andrew eventually would be able to use a token system that provided some type of token (a check mark, a sticker) for steps completed. Then, at the end of all the steps, those marks or stickers would be turned in for his most desired reward (a favorite activity).

In the future, he might be able to respond to a written simple contract, where he would agree to complete certain tasks and we would agree to provide some type of special activity after its completion.

Andrew's educational and home teams were addressing his challenging behaviors of grabbing food, eating nonedibles, pinching, taking his shoes off, tapping objects, and bolting off as well.

Andrew's positive actions were always reinforced with social praise. He would be encouraged to use his words to request, make choices, and reject. Staff would help him request to take a leave instead of bolting off to a desired area.

Parents contributed to our goal planning by completing a form called Steps toward Independence. They identified skills of daily living they believed their son did not have. They were also asked to look into the future and think about where they saw their son living after school, where they thought he might like to work, and in what environments they hoped he could feel comfortable. The Kaplan Foundation then developed goals and action plans to address the areas identified.

Andrew's mom wrote him this letter as his time at the foundation came to a close.

Dear Andrew,

There are two very special rewards of being a parent. One is a child's knowledge of our unconditional love for him. This gives him security and a feeling of being a very special person. The other reward is in watching this child grow into the best person he can be. And at each step toward maturity it is a tremendous joy and relief to watch him finally understand the "whys" of all the rules and lessons that had been laid out for him. With such love and eventual understanding the walk into maturity is made easier.

Dear Andrew, this is what hurts so much about your battle with autism. You had to leave your family and home at such a tender age, and though you were placed in the best care possible filled with love and devotion, you still had to do it alone. We've watched you struggle so hard to achieve the smallest goal, learn the simplest tasks. You have done this all without even knowing the depth of our love for you nor the "whys" to any of it.

And so my son, I can only pray that in some way you can understand how proud your Dad and I and Juliane, Angel, and Joey are of you. Thank you, Andrew. You are a winner!

Love, Mom

50

What heart and courage this mother had all the years she joined hands with the foundation to help give her son the knowledge he would need to have opportunities in his life.

This family never missed a weekend of home time with their son. This family never missed a Special Olympics weekend cheering their son to the finish line. This family never missed a birthday or a holiday to celebrate with their son. This family made weekly phone calls to Andrew at the Kaplan Foundation and they sent letters and cards and special gifts to him to maintain the home connectedness with him.

Never did they fail to send their love and devotion to their son on a daily basis. It is my heartfelt feeling that Andrew knew how his parents felt about him.

Voices of the Families

THERE WERE OTHER VOICES HIDDEN in the large, gray plastic containers in my storage unit, which I uncovered when I made the move from San Rafael to Novato. These were letters and documents families had sent to me when I was gathering information for a book I hoped to write, entitled *The Autism Quilt*.

Andrew's mom sent letters and reports. Kyle's mom sent the Kaplan Foundation newsletters she had saved, as well as individual assessments and individual education plans. There were documents from Marni's mom and letters from Andy and Gail to families and the board of directors. There were newspaper articles that had been written in the early years of the foundation, and there was one red journal notebook from 1980, which Kyle's mom had sent, of my notes to her about his first seven months at the foundation.

The plastic containers held the first employee manuals, sign language manuals, and parent manuals I had developed, meal plans to support healthy development, data sheets for our exercise program, names, addresses, and phone numbers of each child's family I had connected to, copies of residential and educational agreements with districts and regional centers, the first Kaplan Foundation brochures, and touching poems and letters written to sons leaving their mother's care.

As I removed documents from envelopes, unfolded the faded sheets of paper, turned the pages of the newsletters, and remembered the faces of the children, their parents, and their siblings, my emotional state quickly changed from curious to reflective, to thoughtful, to incredibly sad. Tears started streaming down my cheeks. I felt a trembling and realized I was still holding in feelings of loss, which began to pour right out and down my face at that very moment.

Andy and Gail's letter to the board of directors of the Kaplan Foundation and parents of children residing at or attending the day program at the Kaplan Foundation was the piece that brought my stuffed loss pouring out, as I sat on the couch reading its message. The date on the document was July 17, 1998.

The document was entitled "Petition to Reinstate Karen Kaplan as Executive Director of the Kaplan Foundation." I had forgotten all about the letter.

The petition demanded that I immediately be reinstated, that Jim Rogers and Jim Behrman tender their resignations as board members, and that a new board of directors be appointed immediately by the board president, Nyna Cox. At least one of the new directors should be a parent of a child who is a client of the Kaplan Foundation as well.

The petition stated the signers' reasons for making these demands:

> No programs or sites visited by all of us came close to the quality of the Kaplan Foundation. In fact, most had no program other than custodial care. Kaplan is an exception in that capacity. Karen Kaplan provides the energy, vision, and direction for the Kaplan's program.

> Karen Kaplan assured us that under her direction our children would be safe. She personally holds herself responsible. This is extremely rare and very reassuring to us parents.

> Karen Kaplan's expertise and continued hunger for knowledge appeals to the parents.

> The staff is personally trained by Karen Kaplan and thus superior to that of any in other facilities.

> Karen's demand for excellence from both herself and her staff sets Kaplan Foundation apart from the rest.

> Our confidence and trust are in Karen Kaplan. Although the contract reads that our children are clients of the Kaplan Foundation, we have always equated the Kaplan Foundation with Karen Kaplan. We have never encountered someone who advocates for our children as parents do until now.

We are concerned with the reasons Ms. Kaplan was removed so abruptly from her position as executive director. What travesties did she commit to force the board of directors to consider and implement such extreme action? We question why the parents whose lives are directly affected were never consulted or informed that such changes were being contemplated let alone implemented.

A board of directors acting in a responsible, open, and honest manner does not conduct itself or make crucial decisions in the manner that Mr. Rogers or Mr. Behrman has.

There is a "crisis of confidence" at the Kaplan Foundation, and it is not with Karen Kaplan.

I lost something so meaningful back then.

It's like experiencing those nine months to build and nurture a child within you, birthing the child and providing heart, knowledge, and guidance to help it mature, and then losing the child. It's experiencing all those emotional soccer games and watching your child shine on the field and then never seeing another game. It's going through all the amazing stages of your child's motor development: sitting, crawling, learning to stand, and then seeing him finally walk but never seeing him run. It's like seeing your son or daughter graduate from elementary school to middle school and from middle school to high school and then giving your child up for adoption. That was the loss I had stuffed away. That was the loss I was reliving as I read the petition.

But rereading those words reminded me of who I was back then, of who I am today, and of who I have always strived to be: that person who holds herself responsible for her own actions. Yes, I am that person who hungers for knowledge and sets high expectations for herself and those who have worked with her. I have strived to be a trustworthy individual. I have been an advocate and will always be. Thank you, families, for seeing these things in me.

Rereading those words confirms for me how those families felt and the difference I did make in their lives. And while deeply saddened by the loss of the foundation, I am reminded that I was appreciated, valued, and respected. For this, I am grateful.

I remember, wondering, how was it possible that this entity, which I built from my very own hopes, dreams, knowledge, and courage, and with my father's financial support, could be taken away from me in the blink of an eye. I was so naive to think that the Kaplan Foundation was really my school, or that I was the key ingredient to its success, as the parents expressed in their letter.

But as I look back, it didn't matter what role I played at the Kaplan Foundation, or what families or children felt about me, or if the Kaplan Foundation's creation, development, and implementation were due to my dreams, or even if I had been making a difference in anyone's life. I was to be replaced because of someone else's heartlessness, insecurity, and jealousy.

The petition was a great effort made by the families, and I will always be grateful for their belief in me and their attempt to find a way to re-instate me.

I have stayed friends with many of those families and continue to be someone they can trust and count on to advocate for their son or daughter in the future.

Building Community

THE KAPLAN FOUNDATION'S QUARTERLY NEWSLETTER, with the sub-title "A limitless world for the child with autism," began in 1986. It always featured a Teacher's Corner where each teacher highlighted new activities going on in their classrooms. There were also statements celebrating the accomplishments of each student. Then the house notes introduced staff, reported on home activities that the children were engaging in, and reminded readers of up-and-coming parent events and required activities.

Our speech therapist had a page on which she provided information on communication challenges and offered ideas and activities to address them in both school and home environments. Often one of the administrators would add a poem, or I an article that parents could read and find hopeful information about autism. Our meal coordinator always had a page, providing information on nutritional support and special recipes that were being designed to lessen food allergies or sensitivities.

The newsletter always had a Happy Birthday page, sending best wishes to all the children at the foundation, their parents, and their siblings, as well as to our own faculty and staff.

We always kept the families informed if someone was getting married or having a baby, if teachers were coming aboard or moving on, if donations had been made, or if a special event was coming up. A memorial page thanked donors for honoring their love ones by supporting the school.

In the summer of 1986, one of my staff, a young man named Michael Nylander, had passed away. We set up a special fund honoring Michael's time at the school. The funds would purchase special toys, games, and art materials that brought joy and excitement to the students. This is what Michael loved doing with the children.

I will never forget the day Michael's mom called me at the foundation.

He had been in the hospital in a coma for several months. I had made an audiotape of the children and staff talking to him and had brought it to the hospital for the nurses to play to him. I visited Michael several times, telling him all the things that were happening at the school and how much we missed him. Other faculty and staff did the same. Mrs. Nylander had called to ask if I would present the eulogy at the funeral.

I was extremely surprised. I had known Michael for only a year. What I didn't know at the time was that Michael had talked to his family a great deal about working at the Kaplan Foundation and the opportunity given to him to help others. Clearly, the foundation was very important to him. So, I agreed. How does anyone say no to a mother who just lost her son.

I was really nervous, perhaps even a bit frightened by the vision of standing up in the church, in front of his family and friends, casket opened, honoring this young man.

Well, I know it was my heart that said yes, but it was courage I seemed to find that helped me through this very emotional experience. I had not thought about death. I hadn't felt the loss that his mother was going through. How would I find the words to comfort her? Then I found an amazing book written by Dr. Elisabeth Kübler-Ross, *On Death and Dying*. In her book, she describes the stages of grieving that a family goes through. Dr. Kübler-Ross wrote, "Death is simply a shedding of the physical body like the butterfly shedding its cocoon. It is a transition to a higher state of consciousness where you continue to perceive, to understand, to laugh, and to be able to grow." Her writings gave me hope and courage to stand up in front of Mike's family that day.

I was able to say words that I hoped would highlight Mike's contributions at the foundation, honor his caring and compassion for everyone, and express also my optimistic opinion that he is still growing, just on a higher state of consciousness.

I also remembered one letter in the Parents' Corner in the newsletter that truly helped my staff feel valued and appreciated.

Dear Staff,

I would like to take this opportunity to thank all of you for just being there. I know our kids are not the easiest to care for at all times, but you stick with it. You show in so many wonderful ways that you have really taken these kids into your lives and into your hearts. I cannot thank you enough.

When I return my son to Kaplan after his home visit, you help so much by welcoming him with hugs and warm greetings. I feel that you are glad to see him, maybe similar in the way you would greet a good friend you haven't seen for a while. It's a wonderful feeling to know my son has such good friends. I could not ask for anything better.

As you endure the hardships in working with our kids I do know exist, please keep in mind that you are thought of with great admiration and respect for what you do.

Thank you with all our hearts.

Meg Affinito, Kyle's mom

I remember one very special verse that was published in the Parents' Corner of the fall 1991 issue, entitled "What Matters." No author was noted.

> One hundred years from now,
> It will not matter what kind of car I drove
> What kind of house I lived in
> How much I had in my bank account
> Nor what my clothes looked like
> But the world may be a little better because
> I was important in the life of a child . . .

Connie Post, Tom Post's mom and a poet, wrote this poem in August of 1992 and shared it in our winter newsletter that year.

To the Water
> We took a day trip
> To the lake
> Last Saturday.

I rejoiced
Because there were
No tantrums, and no fits.
You and I put our feet
In the lake together.
You were silent
As the ripples of water,
Washed in,
And came to join our party.
The good-byes
That would come
Later that day,
Lay buried beneath
The course gravel,
Under our feet
For that one
Momentary, breezy
Time
All that mattered
Was your feet
And the way
They merged with mine.

In reviewing these newsletters, sent to me and then stored away in the large gray containers, I realized once again that the newsletter celebrated, it informed, it connected the Kaplan Foundation community.

At times the words expressed what so many families were feeling, thus bringing them together and decreasing feelings of isolation and building, I thought, hopefulness.

The Hero's Journey

THOSE WHO TRY TO ACHIEVE deeds on behalf of a group, tribe, or civilization have been said to travel a "Hero's Journey." Scholar and author Joseph Campbell advises us that there are critical elements in telling meaningful stories. He says we witness the Hero's Journey story in many of our key films today, such as *Harry Potter, Lord of the Rings,* and *Star Wars*.

Campbell explains that we learn first about the background of the heroes' lives, then about their "Call to Adventure" when something inside them, or sometimes outside, arises and pushes them forward. The next step often is a "Refusal of the Call," a time of fear of the unknown when a hero may turn away from the path. That is followed by "Meeting the Mentor," beings who represent some external source of wisdom who guide the hero. Next comes "Crossing the Threshold," a time when the hero leaves the ordinary and familiar world and enters the strange and new. There the hero encounters "Tests of Allies and Enemies" and "The Ordeal," a supreme test that carries great fear and the possibility of death. The triumphant hero then receives "The Reward," a treasure for facing the ordeal. Next, the hero begins "The Road Back," the completing of the adventure, and "The Resurrection," the recrossing of the threshold, and "The Climax," the final test. "The Return to Elixir," the culmination of the hero's journey, brings the hero back to his or her community with a magic gift that will benefit all.

I realized that I, too, had been on a Hero's Journey all this time.

The Ordeal

WELL, I MUST SAY, I experienced a few very strong tests on my hero's journey.

In October of 1994 my mother passed away. Her death, from untreatable stomach cancer, placed me in a new category, a category of individuals who have lost a person who had loved them unconditionally. My mom was a tough woman, hard on herself, hard on me, and hard on those around her, but there was no doubt in my mind and heart that she loved me in every way she knew how.

I found myself helping to choose her coffin, writing an obituary, planning an after-burial gathering, and collecting all her personal life items, seeing that they found new homes. I remember sitting on the carpeted hall steps in my parents' home at the after-funeral ceremony, my cousins around me, finally breaking into tears because I would never again taste the sweet raisin kugel she made just for me when I returned from college each school break.

It seemed her death then set off a series of new experiences in my life. My father was alone. I observed him as he followed the traditional Jewish rituals and how he waited one full year before entering into another relationship. One day as we were chatting about his new relationship, he shared that he was happy being with someone who woke up with a smile on her face.

Once again the Wizard spoke and I listened. I realized that my father had stayed with my mother even though he had stopped experiencing that smile. I was following in his footsteps. I was working so hard at being a good mother of three amazing sons, running a residential school for children with autism, and trying to be a loving and supportive wife. But I was failing.

I was alone in my marriage, not by death but by association. I was finally moved to action when my husband chose to have a relationship outside the marriage. The first time it occurred, we separated. The second time, we divorced. A second death. The death of my marriage.

I had been married for nearly twenty years, but not without some bumps in the road, like all marriages. At the ten-year mark, my husband had an affair. Once that was revealed, we separated, I moved out. Then six months later, we were back together trying to recover what we had lost. Both of us agreed our life together was worth another try.

Several years went by, but our marriage was never really the same. He seemed distant. He seemed to be angry with me. Then several challenging conversations occurred, making me realize our marriage was truly over. This time I asked him to leave our home, and we went through the legal process of divorce. I could no longer work with him. I asked the board of directors at the Kaplan Foundation to choose which one of us would continue working for the school.

The directors chose me. I had the expertise in autism, the necessary credentials and training to create program and curriculum, implement evidence-based strategies and interventions, and train the staff and faculty. I also had the knowledge for working with the families, the school districts, and the State Department of Education. My husband was managing maintenance, billing, purchasing, and payroll, all tasks that another operations manager could easily do.

But the anger I sensed wasn't gone. I learned that my husband had obtained an attorney and would be making sure that if he couldn't work at the Kaplan Foundation, neither would I. The board of directors was placed in an awkward position. So they brought in an outside consultant who suggested that the board not only ask him to leave but put me off-site and forbid me contact with any faculty or students' families, if I wanted to maintain my salary and benefits.

The consultant suggested to the board of directors that neither of us was actually needed to run the school. She recommended that new administrators be hired, to avoid the legal accusations made by my husband against the board of directors, and to reduce the current legal challenges they were facing.

Nearly two years after moving through the divorce process and trying to find a way to regain my directorship, I gave in. I was heartbroken, but most of all I was exhausted. I was no longer living my childhood dream. I was playing a legal chess game and each move I made was countered by anger, fear, and jealousy.

Looking back, I was so very naive. I remember my ex-husband saying I lived in a fantasy land. Perhaps he was right. I thought people were generally good and fair. I thought of all the help he and I received from my family when we started our marriage. I thought of all the hardships he had experienced in his life before we met and how supportive he had said I had been. I thought for sure we would be able to work out an amicable divorce agreement.

I was so wrong. I soon realized how much abandonment, anger, and insecurity could affect someone's problem-solving ability. Gratitude, respect, trust, and kindness never entered into the solutions for my soon-to-be-ex-husband.

I remember my last night on the Kaplan Foundation property. I had asked Meg, Kyle's mom, to help me pack up all my materials and equipment from my office. We made sure every piece of program I had developed was in the box I could take home. We made sure every book, article, and curriculum I had bought with my own finances was packed in the trunk of the car. She helped me through that awful day, as I had helped her son at the Kaplan Foundation for seventeen of his twenty-two years of life. She helped me have the courage that night to move forward.

I remember turning out my office light, closing the backdoor to the foundation's administrative offices, and wondering if this was just a bad dream.

I decided to return to school, obtain my administrative credential, and work with my attorney to try to find my way home.

I had run a school for twenty years, but for some reason, like the Scarecrow, I thought I needed a piece of paper to validate my time and experience. I remember thinking, "Was my ex correct? Did I only know autism? And did this mean my abilities were restricted, my next opportunities limited?"

How was it that I could allow one man to have such a huge effect on my self-esteem?

I had made a series of legal attempts, all unsuccessful, to regain the Kaplan Foundation and return to work.

The last straw came when my attorney asked me to give the school notice to vacate. Its lease was up. I took my regular daily walk along the Folsom Lake trail, sobbing, realizing I was not following my dreams, my heart's desire. I was so far away from home it was pathetic. I was not helping others. Then I remembered my dad's words of wisdom. "Do not be possessed by your possessions," he had said. The all-powerful Wizard had spoken.

I asked my attorney that very day to sell my share of the property to the foundation. I was leaving the Land of Kaplan. My ex sold his half with great satisfaction, I assume, knowing he had won.

I remember my attorney handing me the check for my half of the property, commenting that I should feel happy with such a great settlement.

With my eyes filled with tears and my heart broken, I said, "You have no idea how I should feel. I could care less about these dollars. I lost my school, my childhood dream, something I had given twenty years of my life to, and for absolutely no fair reason in the world except one person's anger, insecurity, and jealousy, none of which I deserved, I have lost it."

I was at a fork in the road.

I will say that families and staff continued to contact me, requesting letters of recommendation and recruiting support. Parents asked for help writing their son's or daughter's individual education plans and finding much-needed resources for their children. I never lost contact with many families. They knew I would always be there for them on their road with autism.

The name Kaplan Foundation was removed from the program at my insistence. I updated my résumé and began to put the pieces of my life back together.

I sold the house where we had raised our three boys. Sold the BMW he had suggested we buy and I drove on my fortieth birthday. Sold the beaten-down rental that he had left me as a token of my turning over to him a business my family helped him acquire and that without my signature would never have been his.

On my own I bought a different home in the same school district so my sons would not be uprooted, investing my heart and finances in fixing it up in just the right manner for my next adventure.

The Road Back

I WAS TOLD ABOUT A position as head of school for a private school in Sacramento, Jane Lathrop School, run under the umbrella of the Stanford Home for Children. While I had directed a school, I doubted my ability to run this school as it was for children with severe emotional challenges. But I submitted my application and résumé and was called immediately by the CEO, an amazing man with excellent leadership skills who was well respected in the field. During our first phone conference, I remember telling him that I knew almost nothing about children with emotional challenges, and he said, "Karen, you know how to develop, support, and lead a school. I have confidence you will learn all you need about these children once you take the position." Just like my dad, he saw the abilities I had and gave me the tools to be a successful director for three years.

On Yom Kippur, the Day of Atonement for the Jewish community, I was offered the position. It was one week after the beginning of the Jewish New Year.

Bipolar disorder, conduct disorder, schizophrenia, neglect, and abuse were all highlighted on these students' individual educational plans. Most hated school. Most had failed. Most were embarrassed. All did not trust. Many had probation officers who checked in with them at least quarterly.

My first project was to find a way to get these students to school. I bought a huge barbeque and held Barbeque Monday, which, believe it or not, worked. Food is comfort. Food was the first step for me in establishing a professional relationship with these students. Word traveled fast at the group homes, and soon all students attended school, at least every Monday. In the process of these first meetings, I discovered that my skills, the planned ignoring of inappropriate and negative behaviors and redirecting them, were universal interventions.

My children with autism had trained me well.

My next set of interventions then cinched the deal. The environment I had been asked to improve was in terrible shape. Teachers were disrespectful and boundaries were lacking. I could not ask the students for respect and to respect boundaries if my faculty could not follow these rules. Firing my first teacher and instructional assistant—an act I thought relatively insignificant and natural—changed the entire way the students viewed me. I am sure when the students first saw me walk down the school corridor and be introduced as the new principal, they thought, "What could this five-foot-two-inch white woman possibly know about what we need, who we are, and how to help us?"

I learned very quickly that I was gaining a great deal of respect and trust when I observed new students entering the school. They were quickly put on notice by their peers if they disrespected me. Wow!

I worked with an amazing team at Stanford Home to implement an intensive mental health program at the school. Together, we added counselors to the mix. I hired two additional teachers who were creative and could engage these students. One asked if he could bring drums and other musical instruments to the classroom. Of course, I said yes. The other taught juggling and other circus activities to the students. I hired a third teacher who helped the students believe in their cognitive abilities.

I learned to listen and never to promise something I could not deliver. The school moved from an entrenched environment to a successful educational program with a positive mental health component.

Then came the call. "The Reward" step on the Hero's Journey had arrived. A headhunter asked if I would be interested in interviewing for a head of school position at a school for children with autism in Marin County. I was so excited. I wanted to go back home, home to autism and home to the San Francisco Bay Area. My father was in his eighties, and I also wanted to be close to him.

My eldest son was working, my middle son was on his way to college, and my youngest was ready to leave elementary school—the perfect time to transition to a junior high school in another county. I knew if

I waited any longer, he would not want to move and leave his friends. Going from junior high to high school was the most challenging change for kids, and I knew he wouldn't be able to do it then.

I went through a series of interviews with the Oak Hill School board of directors and with parents and faculty. I accepted the position and gave notice. I would finish my third year at Jane Lathrop and move during the summer to Marin County with my youngest son. I would start as the executive director of Oak Hill just after Labor Day.

I took a huge deep breath and began the steps to move forward. I discussed the adventure with my sons, especially the youngest, as he would be the one impacted. It was agreed he would move with me, attend school in Marin, and see his dad on holidays and some weekends. I put my house in Granite Bay up for sale and on weekends drove to Marin to find its replacement. My house sold quickly, and even though housing options were limited for me in Marin, I found a cute cottage-style home in San Anselmo. All was set. I thought.

Another Test

MY EX AT THE TIME had been living with his girlfriend in Sacramento. My youngest did not want to move into their home or go to a school in Sacramento. He said he would rather live with me. But at the last hour, three weeks before the move, his father said he would rent a house in Granite Bay so my youngest would not have to move. Plans changed.

Although my heart sank into the pit of my stomach once again, I made sure my youngest son knew his choice not to leave his friends was okay. We would figure something out, but I had to leave. My ex would not agree to any collaboration in transporting our son to have contact with me. I even asked him to attend a court-appointed counseling session to see if we could find some type of solution to meet halfway between Sacramento and San Anselmo to exchange Tyler, but he was unwilling to cooperate.

So, every weekend for months I left Marin and booked a room in a hotel so I could spend time with my son. For longer vacations, I drove up to pick him up and drove him back every time. Once he reached the age of fifteen and had confidence enough to take the train on his own, it was a bit easier. When he got his driver's license it was easier still. I drove up for games, proms, and graduation from high school. I know I missed out on some things, but I did my best. I was always available. I made sure not only that his father received the $1,000 a month until my son graduated from high school, but also that he had the clothing he desired, vacations, a laptop for school, and many other necessities for a growing boy. I tried to make every effort for Tyler to know I loved him and was proud of him. When it was time for him to attend college, I made sure his school finances were covered.

Oak Hill School

IN MARIN CITY, TUCKED AWAY on a hillside, was a lovely sea captain's mansion. A white picket fence designated the entrance, and a circular driveway led parents to the students' drop-off and pickup area. One student watched the mileage counter on his mother's car each morning and would not get out of the vehicle until the counter reached a certain number of miles. He coerced his mom into driving around the circle until the numbers lined up.

The school was founded by four families who each had a son on the spectrum of autism. One parent had purchased the property for the school and another financed its huge construction needs, including the lifting of the entire mansion to lay a stronger foundation. These families were committed to developing, building, and supporting a state-of-the-art facility and program for children like their sons.

I came along when the program was struggling. The school was not as yet certified as a California State Department of Education school. In addition, there had been well-intended attempts to direct the school first by the board and then by a faculty member, but it was agreed that outside leadership was needed to take the school to the next level.

My first goals were to complete the certification process, bring the faculty and staff together, and find ways to develop a positive relationship with other schools in the county. It was also part of my work to identify other sources of revenues to sustain the school.

Within three years, all these goals were met. We became a highly recognized school. Because 90 per cent of our students were placed by the public school districts, we no longer were solely dependent on private school funding or donations. Our teachers and therapists were collaborating well, and others in the field were interested in working at Oak Hill.

In this time, I had remodeled the building at least twice, gone through the necessary process with the city to add a portable classroom, and worked with the board to put on annual fundraising events. I had developed relationships with other schools, so a few of our students could have typical peer interactions. We were offering drama therapy and creative arts therapy. And we were growing. We had moved from eleven students to twenty-two students. I was very proud that our founders no longer had to write checks to cover the daily operations.

I remember each day standing at the top of the steps greeting my students, watching them eagerly run to get to their classrooms. Our students wanted to come to school. They were happy to see their teachers, who had taken the time to help them feel safe and to identify their interests so that they could learn. They were happy to get into their classrooms, where they could sit on balls or jump on mini-bouncers if needed to calm their bodies in order to engage in learning.

Teachers set up structured classrooms, with visual schedules to support our students' limited executive functioning ability. They used meaningful and purposeful activities to teach.

For example, students discovered knowledge, communication strategies, and coping strategies when engaging with our creative arts therapist in art activities, musical activities, and movement activities. They developed their fine motor and motor planning skills by drawing, cutting, gluing, assembling, tying, and so on. Students developed better balance, strength, sensory integration, and gross motor skills by working with the occupational therapist on-site. Students who were anxious about going to the doctor or riding in an airplane met with the drama therapist and enacted those activities so they would be better able to handle the event when it actually occurred. Teachers would develop visual Social Stories containing solutions to address students' anxieties that could be read over and over again to prepare them for these sensitive activities.

We created fun and engaging events to teach our students how to join their peers in a well-known community celebration.

The entire mansion vibrated when Lizzy played the built-in organ to announce the Halloween parade and assembly. Those eerie notes echoed throughout the two-story building with its dark, wooden wainscoting. Students in their costumes came out of their classrooms into the large living room, which had been converted to a classroom, to participate in the assembly. Lizzy had worked with older students, creating songs for the holiday. There was a song that taught how to knock on doors and utter those magical words "Trick or treat." When the parade started, several of us hid behind our closed office doors. We waited for the knock before opening. Then we waited again for those special words "Trick or treat" before we would hand out a treat. Then the students would move on to the next closed door.

Through their participation in school assemblies for Halloween, Valentine's Day, and winter holidays, our students learned social and communication skills and developed positive self-esteem. The most impressive assembly was our annual Thanksgiving Feast. Lizzy, our creative arts therapist, made a Thankful Tree. Students wrote something they were thankful for on a large leaf and hung it on the tree. They participated in all the food preparing, table setting, and decorating. Then we had visitors! Three of our faculty dressed up as visiting family members, to the delight of the students. The costumes were amazing. Uncle Joe and Aunt Charla would come and display very rude and antisocial behavior. The students would love identifying what they were doing wrong and offer them better social suggestions. Lots of giggling that day.

This one-day feast helped our students learn how they should behave in their own homes during their very own Thanksgiving event in a fun, playful, and meaningful manner.

Lizzy taught me to be playful and to tap into my creative ability. One day, I asked my executive assistant if she would help me play "In & Out Burger." I had bought T-shirts and obtained those paper hats the workers wore at In & Out. My office was a perfect burger place. First, I had two huge windows that looked out on the playground. So we labeled one "Order" and the other, "Pickup." We called In & Out and ordered vanilla and chocolate milkshakes, French fries, plain burgers, and cheeseburgers, enough for the staff and students. We did not tell anyone. While the students were in their classrooms almost ready to come out for recess before lunch, I called the teachers and told them I needed to see them once their students were at recess. So now I had everyone coming downstairs. My assistant went and picked up all the goodies. We set up our burger stand. We were ready for their orders.

My teachers, concerned about my phone call, were all smiling once they saw what we had set up. The students had to use their communication skills at the first window to place their order and then their social skills to say thank you at the pickup window. It was a memorable day for all at Oak Hill School!

My Oak Hill days were filled with opportunities to connect with my heart, have the courage to make changes, and continue acquiring knowledge and offering knowledge to help my faculty, the students, and their families.

The Resurrection

THEN CAME "THE RESURRECTION" STAGE of the Hero's Journey. Certainly, what I hoped would be my final test. My father passed away. I have never been so devastated in my life as that December 1st when I entered my father's house early in the morning and saw the two hospice women sitting on the bench at the top of the stairs, with their backs against the wall. I had just shouted out "Dad, I'm here" when the dark-haired hospice woman said, "I am so sorry, your Dad just passed away." I am not sure if my scream was heard through the thin walls of the neighbors' homes, but it was definitely heard by those two petite women.

I knew my dad was in the final stages of his ninety years, but I had just sat with him the night before, discussing his thoughts about my need to date once again. I knew his exhausted heart was struggling to keep him alive. I knew that when he could no longer get to the 49ers games and assume his season-ticket holder's seat, he was ready to leave the physical world. He had told me that he had lived a long life and that he was ready, but I had never truly accepted the fact he would not be physically with me in my life.

How could this person who truly—I mean truly—demonstrated unconditional love no longer be there to guide and support and love me? I had lost my mom, gone through a difficult divorce, lost my school, moved away from daily contact with my youngest son. And now my Sundays with Max, enjoying conversation and watching him place that over-easy egg on top on his waffle, or stirring spoonfuls of apricot jam into his Lipton tea—those days were over. No more new Wizardly advice.

I really do not remember the exact details of the next six months. I know that I planned the funeral, a Masonic funeral. I know that I called for the company to come retrieve the medical equipment we had purchased to make him comfortable those last couple of months. I know that I went with my brother to Dick Greene's office to hear the reading of the will. I remember sitting in my dad's home crying, as I prepared the house for my cousin to use the next year. Her son was going through medical treatments at the University of California, San Francisco, and my dad's home could provide some love and support.

I remember going to work each day at Oak Hill and hoping I would not hear a song on the radio that would fill my eyes with tears. But I don't remember many of the details until Spring Break when I took a trip to Sedona. Little did I know that this trip would allow me to return home and continue the journey.

My trip to Sedona provided opportunities each day to grieve and re-member wonderful memories of my dad. My father was an avid Western novel reader. His favorite authors were Louis L'Amour and Max Brand. One of his favorite movies was *Lost Horizon*, which took place in Shangri La. My dad held positions in the Masons and Easter Star Organizations. He went out of his way to find a comfortable high-back chair to sit in while falling asleep each night watching his favorite shows or enjoying the 49ers on TV.

The activity center that organized my trips around Sedona was called Shangri La. My first excursion took me to the desert where Louis L'Amour and Max Brand got the inspiration to write their books. A walk through another part of Sedona Hills landed me directly next to an old Masonic Temple and finally to a huge rock formation in the side of the mountain with a high-back chair embossed in it.

Odd, unexpected, coincidental, who knows, perhaps just serendipitous. I was able to release the last six months of holding in all my feelings.

I was able to return to Oak Hill and complete my journey there and take some big steps needed in my life.

Oak Hill School was looking to take a different direction. The board felt they were ready for international recognition and needed to change my position to one that I felt didn't really use the strengths I had. We agreed that I would give nine months' notice and they would begin searching for my replacement.

An Important Mentor for Thinking Bigger: The Yellow Brick Road Leads to Bali

I HAD BEGUN WORKING WITH a mentor during my last year at Oak Hill School, and with her guidance, I chose to take a year off from directing any kind of school or working for another organization. Since Oak Hill was going in a different direction, I would seize the opportunity to discover more about my next call to adventure. I had never made a choice like this. I had always planned the next adventure before I took the leap.

A friend referred me to Agnes. She had a gift for helping people. Agnes was able to confirm that I was meant to teach, but she said it was time to Think Bigger, to think about traveling east, and to write.

She and I met quarterly. She suggested some books to read, tapes to listen to, and we explored how I might expand my thinking about my next steps on the road. She didn't have a crystal ball, but like the fortune teller Dorothy met, she had great wisdoms and helped me move forward on my journey.

First I chose to do some traveling and self-exploration. I think Dorothy's travel to the Land of Oz was certainly about self-exploration.

I traveled a bit, did some long-needed reading for pleasure and development, and joined in the founding of the Marin Autism Collaborative. I added more private consulting. During this time, I also founded the Marin Autism Lecture Series and facilitated this important project until May of 2016 when the seventh series came to an end. Researchers, scientists, authors, therapists, educational specialists, medical practitioners, and finally the voices of those living on the autism spectrum presented at these lectures.

Then I founded a nonprofit called Offerings, creating a viable 501(c)(3) with a caring board of directors to raise money to put on the series.

I also developed the North Bay Autism Resource Fair, which provided a one-stop venue for families to access autism resources. This event was also supported under the nonprofit.

I also taught for Alliant University in San Francisco in its credentialing program and helped it and other universities to develop their autism authorization certification required for teaching children on the spectrum.

If you remember, the film version of *The Wizard of Oz* opens with Dorothy trying to find something to do on the farm, but she keeps getting in everyone's hair and is told to get out of the way. She begins to feel as if she doesn't belong, she has no home. So she decides to pack her things and run away.

She heads out, unaware that a tornado is approaching. Soon she comes upon a traveling Gypsy Wagon that is pulled off the side of the road and notices the sign on the wagon that says "Fortune Teller." The fortune teller asks Dorothy to explain why she is out on the road alone. She explains that she is leaving home. He sits down and looks into his crystal ball and lets Dorothy know that her Aunt Em is missing her and is very sad and worried about her.

Dorothy gets the message and heads for home, but as we all know, she finds no one in the house and is then hit over the head and knocked out. Later she awakens to find that her house has been traveling inside a tornado, and soon she ends up in the Land of Oz. She is no longer in Kansas.

There was indeed a little tornado stirring each time I left Agnes's office. I did find my mind spinning and, believe it or not, I soon found myself in a faraway land.

Much like Dorothy's discoveries along the Yellow Brick Road, in the beginning my adventures in Bali seemed to happen quite organically. I had been sending money to a nongovernmental organization called Yayasna Kemanusiaan Ibu Pertiwi (YKIP) that provided educational support to children on the island, who otherwise would not have a chance to attend school. I supported a young girl named Komang.

I researched the nonprofit and found that it was associated with another nongovernmental organization that helped children and adults with physical challenges, and I discovered that it had a small center providing education and therapy to the children. I sent my résumé to the director of YPK (Yayasna Peduli Kemansian; in English: Bali Humanity Care Foundation), the center for the physically challenged, and asked if I might visit while on the island. Not only did the director encourage me to visit but inquired if I might sit with his teachers and talk about special needs. I agreed, and my teaching was on its way to Bigger!

I found the Balinese to be a kind and caring people and very family-oriented. In many ceremonies they wear black and white, perform interesting dances, and burn incense. Some Balinese still visit shamans to find answers to illness and to set auspicious dates for marriages, building houses, and opening businesses.

Agnes's predictions were right, confirming that teaching was on my road with autism and on my chart of life. For all of you now raising your eyebrows, let me just confirm that Agnes had been spot-on with so many things before. She had this amazing ability to look at the moment I was born and see what it meant beyond a simple yearly birthday celebration.

Six years before I first took the road to Bali, she had asked me to Think Bigger and go east, perhaps to the island of Bali, where Elizabeth Gilbert, author of *Eat Pray Love*, found her way.

Well, after seven trips to Bali in six years, teaching in small nongovernmental schools and centers for the disabled, all I can say is that her words of wisdom had great meaning in my life. You might still be raising your eyebrows! But believe it or not, there was a real yellow road, a street called Jalan Raya, in Ubud, Bali, that I walked on the six years I spent in Bali, exploring, learning, and teaching.

My time in Bali helped me realize I needed to create my nonprofit Offerings, which provided education, knowledge, resources, and mentoring locally and globally to parents, grandparents, teachers, therapists, administrators, medical practitioners, university students, and those who live each day on the autism spectrum.

My life certainly got bigger as I learned how to teach in different lands with different sets of beliefs, values, and practices.

I also learned that when a mother, father, aunt, grandmother, sister, brother, or those professionals wanting to make a difference gained knowledge, understanding, and resources, true solutions could be found. I knew that grief, depression, anger, and desperation decreased when one had solutions, whether one lived in America or Indonesia or anywhere else in the world.

Yuni, My Glinda

AFTER THE ENCOURAGEMENT FROM THE director of YPK, I bought my airline tickets, reserved my bungalow in the city of Ubud, updated my tetanus vaccination, and read three books to help me begin to understand the culture, beliefs, and gifts of the island.

My relationship with YPK grew mostly from the wonderful connection I was able to develop with a beautiful young Balinese student who was completing her regular teaching credential at the local college on the island. Wahyuni Andhitya, or Yuni, was the lead teacher at YPK. Open to learning, she hungered for knowledge. She was committed to and passionate about making a difference in the lives of those children who came to receive therapy at the center. A very wise director at YPK had chosen her to take on the leadership role at the center. She had many wonderful new ideas and wanted to offer much more to the children and families.

I often took my lead from Yuni and developed workshops based on what she and her supervisor saw as needed to expand the knowledge at YPK. Yuni became my translator as well, taking my words and putting them into Bahasa Indonesian, helping those with less English understand more at workshops. Yuni was instrumental in organizing our annual special needs collaboration seminar at the Annika Linden Centre in Denpasar, Bali. She was my on-the-ground coordinator and friend. Later in our relationship, Yuni traveled with me to Jakarta, where together we presented to nearly three hundred people at a daylong conference hosted by the Indonesia Autism Society, discussing how to create a program for children with autism.

YPK was located in the business center in Denpasar, Bali, about one hour from Ubud, where I was staying. It was an NGO (nongovernmental organization) largely funded by the Annika Linden Foundation, known today as Inspirasia. The story goes that Annika Linden was a young woman killed in the 2002 Bali bombings whose fiancé wanted to create something to honor her life.

Yellow-and-blue linoleum squares lined the floors of YPK's first site. On the bottom floor of the center was a room with physical therapy equipment, a bathroom, and two tiny office spaces designating the school. Up a flight of stairs was the tiny office of the director, his teachers, a marketing volunteer, and the visiting occupational therapist. A small wooden playground structure was outside the front doors of the center.

I remember the first day of my visit, all the smiles and warm feelings of welcome. This was the very day I met Yuni. Bali was her home, and she had been raised as an educated Balinese woman. Yuni was filled with a promise of possibilities. She believed in the potential of these children. The director of YPK, Pak Purnawan, believed in her. He, too, was wise, caring, and openhearted, hoping to change the lives of those with challenges and their families.

The children at the center spent time with a physical therapist or occupational therapist and also in one of the two small rooms, where they were offered knowledge not otherwise available to them because they were not permitted to attend the mainstream education system. These children had cerebral palsy challenges, attention-deficit/hyperactivity diagnosis, cognitive delay, seizures, or a mix of development and physical differences found on the island.

Yuni wanted to know how to work with these children in a group because, owing to limited funding, the center couldn't provide one-on-one support. I asked if we could get the children, six of them, in a circle with appropriate supports for their physical challenges. I asked if she had any musical instruments.

She took me down a narrow hallway into a backroom and a dark closet filled with an assortment of odds and ends, unused equipment, and, at last, some musical instruments—bamboo shakers. Perfect. Her support teachers positioned all the boys in a circle facing each other. We handed each boy a bamboo shaker. I became the group's first leader and showed the teachers how they might get group responses from these very different children. I could not speak a word of Balinese but had a great deal of hope. My plan worked. The support staff helped the students match my actions, first repeating the number of shakes to facilitate counting, then directing the shakers to facilitate directionality, and then varying volume and speed, continuing to build concept understanding. I next asked Yuni to become the leader and repeat. Then I asked a student to be a leader and show us a motion, and we copied. We went around the circle asking each student to lead.

Then I named a category (animals), and each of us took a turn shaking the instrument and naming our favorite animal. "Let's name these animals and shake to the syllables of the animals' names: mon-key, li-on, cow, al-li-ga-tor," I suggested. I followed with the categories of colors and transportation, and Yuni and the teachers saw how, with a simple instrument, they could teach children to build concepts, numbers, categories, imitation, and turn taking and get group involvement with limited support.

They were hopeful. I was grateful for the opportunity to teach. I was full.

Yuni and Sharon, an occupational therapist from Australia, then invited me upstairs to the small administrative office. The director made me some of his very special tea and we talked about my work in California. Yuni asked if I would stay a bit longer and meet with the teachers and talk to them about autism, a very new subject to them. They were curious.

I had prepared a simple PowerPoint on autism before leaving home, just in case. I spent the next hour trying to communicate with this group of passionate teachers whose knowledge of English was very limited. I guess my ability to use my hands and body and facial gestures helped. But Yuni had been speaking English for some time so she began her translation of my work that very day.

Over the next seven visits in six years, my relationship with the YPK center grew and grew, and for the next year and years following, Yuni and I worked together to bring centers to her new site, to share and learn in a day of discussions and presentations. Yuni translated all my English words into Bahasa Indonesian, so as to truly support our guests' learning and their feelings of connectedness. Teachers, therapists, administrators, and families joined our yearly seminar, building a positive network that stayed connected even after I returned to America.

In the summer of 2016, there were many moments that confirmed that for six years I had been on the right Yellow Brick Road in Bali. But one remarkable moment showed me the impact one person, myself this time, could have on changing how children with special needs were understood.

I was presenting on cerebral palsy, discussing its causes and interventions, at a three-part workshop helping teachers and parents understand autism, Down syndrome, and cerebral palsy. Always, at the end of each workshop I facilitate, I ask each guest to tell me one new thing he or she has learned. One mom, a staff person at a local center for children with developmental challenges who had a son with autism, said, "I learned that cerebral palsy is not about a broken arm but about a challenge occurring in the brain which affects the arm."

I realized, at that moment, that just one piece of information I passed on would be shared with others and that this information would affect the way a teacher or parent understood how to help, teach, and support a child with CP.

If nothing else of importance happened during my time in Bali during the summer of 2016, I was okay. It's those precious little moments in one's life that often become the most meaningful.

The Courage to Take a Ride

THE INTERNET IS AN AMAZING connector. Before my first trip to Bali, while cruising through autism and Bali sites, I found a posting that caught my attention. A Balinese man wanted to open a school for children with autism. He didn't appear to have any experience, but heart and courage came through in his postings. So, I contacted him and let him know I would be coming to Bali and would be happy to share my experience and knowledge. We agreed to try to connect when I arrived.

With my son, who accompanied me on my first visit to Bali, I found the courage to take a ride to the young man's village. We had no idea where we were going, no idea who this young man truly was, but just like the Tin Man and the Scarecrow, we were up for an adventure. The young man had explained that he hoped to add on space to his own home and use it to help families in his village who had children with autism. He and his wife and two children already lived in the home, but they wanted to make a difference.

We arrived at the village and walked a short distance to this young man's home. My son and I realized that the village was incredibly poor and that the space being added on was about as big as a small carport.

A pile of rocks lay in the corner of the future learning environment. Later this pile of rocks helped me connect a ten-year-old boy with a couple of his local typical peers who had come to observe me this very day.

Komang was the first child with autism I met in Bali. Yes, Komang again, a name I soon found that was given to all second-born children in a specific caste in Bali. His mother brought him to the home to meet me. He was impeccably clean and held a Spider-man figure in his hand. My young Balinese man hoped I would have some words of wisdom to help him teach Komang.

Komang's mother found my face immediately and smiled, while

Komang's eyes never met mine or anyone else's when he entered the home. He seemed to feel very comfortable in this home and asserted control immediately, walking right through the space soon to be his school, straight into the house, past two small bedrooms and a kitchen, through the dining room and the living room, directly to the bookshelf.

Okay, I thought, what next? He has said nothing. He didn't even acknowledge my presence and I am hard to miss—the only white-haired woman in his environment. His family speaks Balinese to him and I haven't one word of Balinese in my repertoire.

Komang gave me my opening. He began to remove books from the shelves and toss them one at a time on the floor, never taking a moment to stop, open a book, or engage with a single page. No one gave him any type of direction, but they stood there waiting to see what I would do. So, I picked up each book immediately after he tossed it on the floor and returned it to the shelf.

No response on the first three returns. Then it happened, my first glance from Komang and a little furrow in his forehead. Perhaps he was wondering what this short, white-haired woman was doing interrupting his highly repetitive activity. He continued to toss and I continued to return.

Then instead of returning the book to the shelf on my own, I offered the book to Komang, hoping he might enter into something reciprocal with me, joining our attention. Nope, he just stopped tossing and sat down. Me, too.

A box of blocks sat next to the bookshelf. Komang proceeded to empty the box and begin to build. Okay, I thought, another opening. I then moved the stack of blocks farther and farther away from Komang, protecting them with my body. My intention was to try to join his activity in hopes he would share this experience with me. Soon Komang ran out of blocks to add to his structure. I held out one and he accepted it. After a couple of acceptances, he even glanced in my direction, waiting for me to hand him the next block. He let me join his play, block after block, until we had made an amazing structure. Then I found some toy cars and started moving them through the structure, making car noises. Komang smiled and laughed and we truly connected. Komang tried

90

some of the toy cars and then got up and walked outside still holding on to Spider-man.

Once outside, I started singing the theme from *Spider-man* and Komang smiled again.

Several children were playing outside in the pile of stones. Disregarding the children, Komang went over to the pile and sifted the stones through his hands. I interrupted and said no, the first no I think anyone had said to him. The others seemed confused by my action.

I showed Komang how to use a shovel and fill up the buckets with stones and then pour them out, giving him a different way of sifting stones. He refused to imitate my actions and tried sifting the stones again. I repeated my no and physically put his hands through the steps. After a couple more nos and modeling, Komang matched my actions and joined the others at the pile of stones.

The driver who took us to the village that day also hoped to become the head teacher of the school. I explained to him that one way of connecting with children was to join them first in their own actions and then carefully obstruct and expand into new actions. He joined Komang at the pile, shaped and modeled, and had his first experience in teaching. He was hopeful and grateful.

Komang's mother thanked me and let me know that Komang's older brother was also someone on the autism spectrum, and that he was known by all as the very best cement mixer in the village. I smiled, once again reminded of how important it is to identify the gifts, talents, and interests of all individuals and to help them discover whatever they are best at.

My son and I were driven back to our bungalows. I was grateful for the opportunity to have met Komang, his mom, and a very special driver.

Differently Abled Stories

THERE WAS ANOTHER INTERESTING EXPERIENCE on my first trip to Bali that helped me connect to the world of special needs. I was out strolling through the streets of Ubud and ventured down one of the main roads, Monkey Forest Road. There I noticed a large painting on the front of a yellow stucco building next to the soccer field. It was a caricature of a boy with outstretched wings. Below were the words "Mentally Disabled." I was surprised but drawn to the space.

As I approached the building and went through the archway, the words "Differently Able," painted on a wooden board hanging across the entrance, put a smile on my face. Inside were some tables and a kitchen, making the building look somewhat like a café. There was a very large open space with some climbing equipment in the center. Stairs led up to an enclosed balcony, where I later learned were two classrooms. There appeared to be a small library and a little art gallery with items for sale.

I peered in and a voice shouted, "Karen Kaplan, what are you doing in Bali?" Serendipitous or just a coincidence, a young lady I had recently met in California at one of my special needs resource fairs was standing upstairs on the balcony. She was an occupational therapist at a local school in San Carlos, just a couple of exits up from the school I was directing in Redwood City. Small world.

She shared how she was volunteering at Sakjartarius Center, and I shared I was vacationing and learning about special needs on Bali. She introduced me to the Balinese director of the center, and I collected information about the founders. I later used that information to meet the founders themselves, who were from Holland and had a daughter with Down syndrome.

On my next trip to Bali, I returned to Sakjartarius Center and met with the teachers and staff to discuss how to use music therapy with

special needs children to expand communication, teach group participation, and develop positive social and emotional skills. The director
of Sakjartarius later joined our collaborative meetings at the Annika
Linden Centre and brought her teaching staff.

I was traveling on my own road in Bali, and as it happened to Dorothy in
the Land of Oz, my name was being passed on to others and my adventures were being shared with related communities. I was asked to present
at the Rotary Club, which met once a month on Monday evenings in
Ubud. The group wanted to learn how autism was growing in the world
and how it was affecting children and families.

The owner of Juice Java, a local Ubud business, who attended that
evening, asked if I would meet with the founder of Sari Haiti, a special needs center about fifteen minutes by motorbike from my hotel.
I agreed. I connected with Tanja at Casa Luna, a restaurant across the
street from my bungalow, off the main street in Ubud. The first time I
met her, she arrived on her motorbike. Tanja was this wonderful woman
from Switzerland who had married a Balinese man. She not only was
raising three children of her own on the island but was active in the
establishment and sustainability of Sari Haiti Center.

She and I hit it off that day, and I hopped on the back of her motorbike
that very first meeting and went to see Sari Haiti. This is where I met
Sari Pollen, a young woman born in Bali who was leading the teaching
staff and establishing the program for children with Down syndrome,
cerebral palsy, intellectual disabilities, ADHD (attention-deficit/hyper-
activity disorder), and autism at the center.

I was so impressed by the passion I witnessed that day. Sari Pollen was
facilitating a yoga session with the support of one of the children at the
center, who herself had a learning disability. Then Sari led a drumming
and singing group with twenty of the children. The smiles on those
young faces were as wide as the Cheshire Cat's in *Alice's Adventures in
Wonderland*. I also happened to be on-site during ceremony hour and
watched a young lady with Down syndrome light incense, move her
hands in a waving fashion after dipping flowers in holy water, and complete the afternoon offerings of gratitude. My heart was full that day.

Tanja and Sari met with me afterward. We decided I would return, listen to the challenges the teachers were facing, and provide suggestions on how to work with some of the more difficult children. The teachers and staff at Sari Haiti also joined the Annika Linden Centre collaborations during my future visits to Bali. Sari, Tanja, and I worked together from that day forward, addressing challenges as the center grew and changed.

During one of my Internet-browsing experiences on autism and Indonesia, I saw that there was a school for children with autism in Denpasar. I asked Yuni if she knew of the school and if there was a way we might visit. Yuni made the connection. I sent my résumé once again to the director and was invited.

I asked Yuni and Sharon, her occupational therapist, if they would like to join me. Pak Purnawan, the director of YPK, also wanted to go with us, and so a date was scheduled. My niece, an educational specialist in Marin County, traveled with me that year to help present at our first collaboration at the Annika Linden Centre, hosted by YPK. She, too, went with us to the autism school.

We expected to tour the site and meet with just the staff for an informal discussion. But our experience was very different that day. First, a reception line greeted me. I was honored. Then, thirty of the children were asked to come to the center that day for me to see. Wow, unexpected. Next I was told that all the families and members of the village who were interested in the center would be coming, and I would be addressing them. Double Wow! You can only imagine the look on our faces when we heard the event schedule.

Well, with my heart beating, my brain expanding, and my badge of courage shiny, I walked through the center's front doors and followed the director of the program to the gym, where the thirty children with autism were waiting. All I could think of was the children's sensory overload or anxiety that we might see.

On the way to the gym, I asked the director about her background. She said she was a veterinarian. I then asked her if she had a child with autism in her family. She responded no. Finally I asked her how it was that she ended up directing a school for children with autism, and she said there was a need in her village.

I asked the team to wait outside the gym door for a few moments while I peeked in. Thirty-plus children with special needs were wandering around or sitting on the blue and yellow mats in the gym. No structured activities were going on. One young girl in the corner definitely was overwhelmed, hitting her head. Her distressed noises were my sign that having a group come in and tour in this room was not the right choice.

As I turned to walk out, I scanned the entire space. Although I had no diagnostic information with me to know for sure what their disabilities were, I knew they were not all children with autism. I saw several children with Down syndrome and perhaps a few with genetic or additional physical or intellectual challenges.

I suggested the tour continue on. I was shown some small teaching rooms, rooms that looked much like our small one-on-one, discrete-trial-system rooms, and then a small room where a speech therapist was working with a seventeen-year-old student with autism on oral motor work. I saw a few more rooms that were used for teaching and then was taken into a large assembly room where I was to now address the entire community. No children.

On that walk to the assembly room, I was trying to absorb what I had just seen and heard and to think about how I might address fifty-plus adults. They had arranged the room assembly-style fashion, with an eight-foot table on the stage for me to sit at, higher than the guests. Some bottled water waited for me. A box of treats as well, the last thing I needed at this time. I was delighted to sip the water and gather my thoughts. I asked to sit closer to the guests, on the stage floor rather than at the table, to be more at eye level with them.

My team took seats in the front row, thank goodness. I had to ask Yuni for translating help, as the young man they assigned to translate was not as effective in translating autism information as everyone had hoped.

I was introduced, or at least my credentials were. It was the day I heard the word "Guru" attached to my name. I giggled, only to realize later it simply meant teacher and I was certainly that.

I thanked the director of the school for inviting us, and I honored those who had set up this center for children with autism and other special needs. I told them more about my background and experience and my current work in America.

I kept thinking, "Listen. Do not judge. Be honest. Do not destroy hope." This became my mantra from that day forward.

We decided that day that the guests could ask me any questions they had on their minds and I would make every effort to provide helpful information.

Question 1: What is autism?

Question 2: Can children with Down syndrome be educated in the same school?

Question 3: What medication cures autism?

Question 4: Is it okay to throw my son in water when he is having a tantrum?

These were just the first four questions.

Listen. Do not judge. Be honest. Do not destroy hope. My mantra played over and over again in my mind as I processed these questions.

Answering the first question about autism was the easiest, but doing so in a way that related to the local culture took time. I tried to describe and give examples that those fifty villagers could understand, going slowly enough so the translators could reframe my examples if necessary.

I needed to reframe the next question so that the director and the teachers didn't lose face. I was able to help them understand the similarities between autism and Down syndrome, and then I helped them see the difference between the two so that the school could design additional education and therapeutic strategies for each.

The father who had asked the third question looked so sad. I could see him hanging on to the hope that I might say he could give his son something that would enable him to be just like other villagers' sons. I let this dad know that some medications might help improve some of the symptoms (attention, anxiety, and obsessiveness), but at this time researchers and scientists had not yet found a medication that cures autism. I didn't want him to lose hope.

The mother who stood up in front of her village that day and asked if it was okay to throw her son in water when he had a tantrum had such courage. I wanted to answer her question carefully so as not to embarrass her in front of her peers and to show I wasn't judging her.

I asked this mother to tell us the story that led up to her son's tantrum. I listened so carefully, trying to find some cue that would tell me how this mother could help her son avoid getting to the tantrum stage. We talked about our children's lack of understanding of time (waiting is hard). We talked about preparing our children for change and new experiences (to decrease anxiety). We talked about the importance of developing a communication system for these children (to express their needs, wants, and feelings). Then I asked her if her son enjoyed the water and explained how water can often help some children to calm and re-center. She said no, he did not enjoy water. I then shared that sometimes offering something children disliked could help change a behavior, but if something was fearful to the child, then it was really important to try everything else first and avoid things the child feared.

After six hours of questions and answers, I was ready to be silent. Hours of listening, waiting for translations, processing and remembering my mantra, to be honest, to pass no judgment, and never to destroy hope, before responding all had to come to completion for the day. I hoped that I had offered a tiny bit of help. I hoped I hadn't destroyed the father's hope. I hoped that the mother who had tossed her frightened child in the water would be able to use one or more of the strategies I offered.

The director and her team hoped I would return.

I remember sitting in the van, emotionally exhausted, staring out the window at the rows of motorbikes with families traveling somewhere, wishing I could just stay for a year to help mentor this caring and committed community.

Deepening Bali Connections

IN THE LAND OF BALI, I felt different. Perhaps this island's customs, its people, its pace, its climate, and its calling affected me.

In Bali, it was acceptable for me to sit in a café for hours, reading, writing, and engaging in conversation with others. Being in Bali allowed me to see the colors of the people and their lives. It gave me an opportunity to just stop, address my physical wellness, and wonder. It allowed me to imagine. It allowed me to see life lived in a different way. An escape, maybe. Whatever it was, it drew me back for six years, this Land of Bali.

With some wisdom, a great deal of heart, and the courage to say yes, I continued to reach back to people and programs on the island that wished to learn. With the help of Yuni from YPK, the Annika Linden Centre became the host of many collaborations.

It is important to understand that on Bali, life is centered in the village. All families living within the village work together for its positive spiritual and business health. Collaboration between villages, however, is not automatic. So, when I first arrived, the special needs programs that I would encounter were not meeting and problem-solving together. I suggested to Yuni that we invite any and all centers to a gathering. Each center would present its program, I would present on a key topic of interest to the centers, I would facilitate the group in sharing challenges and solutions, and finally we would build community by partaking in a meal together.

At the first collaboration, my niece talked about how she became a teacher in the public schools and what the education system was like in California. My psychologist colleague shared about her role with special children in the United States. My teacher colleague from a local California autism school shared her education and experience as a teacher as well.

My topic for the collaboration was how to use cooking to address academic, social, motor, and communication challenges in children with special needs. The day was a wonderful beginning of future collaboration between faculty and staff. I was very proud to have been a part of this.

As a teacher in the Land of Bali, I learned to ask the people what they needed. I was careful to always remember that the American Way may not be realistic, possible, or aligned with the values in the land. I learned to honor and respect the culture. I learned I must create a safe learning environment where people were not afraid to ask questions. I had to remember that a head shake yes did not always mean someone understood. I needed to check for understanding.

During my seven trips to Bali, the centers asked to learn about autism and ADHD. They wanted to know how to handle behavioral challenges. We discussed their need to become detectives or act like doctors who look at all their patients' symptoms, to identify how behaviors develop. They yearned for alternative educational approaches. They wondered how to integrate children with special needs into regular classrooms. They hadn't heard of functional-based curriculums. They wanted to know how to teach with their limited resources. They wanted to understand how to help children communicate, follow directions, and become independent.

We talked about how to support the siblings of children with special needs. We discussed how to set up life skill and prevocational programs. I also suggested different ways to think about the integration and admission of typical students with special needs.

We discussed how to address the wellness of families and professionals and ways to fundraise in centers. I was able to bring information to them on sensory integration, the communication challenges of those with autism, and alternative communication systems.

A Very Proud Mom

THE LAND OF BALI PROVIDED another opportunity that truly deepened my understanding of those with special needs and acceptance.

I was given three amazing sons in this life. During the years in the Land of Bali, they joined me in giving.

My son Joshua took the lead. It was through his knowledge and experience that I could even dream of using the sport of soccer to create a day of acceptance, belonging, and understanding. Joshua had played soccer ever since he could walk. As a matter of fact, his dad and I placed a small soccer ball in his crib. He took to soccer like a fish to water and played at every level possible all the way through high school. Then he proceeded to add rugby to his skill set and played and coached through college and beyond.

The first soccer day in Bali started with a group of teens from the organization to which I had for several years pledged educational support, so that teens from families with limited resources could attend school. Forty teens enjoyed a special day moving through soccer drills with a licensed coach from America and went home not only with a soccer ball and a jersey in their hands but with huge smiles on their faces.

Then it happened. The soccer day became the bridge between the typical children and children with special needs. Josh's two younger brothers joined him in giving children who had never been on the soccer field, never played side by side with typical children, and never had their own soccer ball the opportunity to play with typical teens from the organization I had supported. Wheelchairs moved through drills. Children with bodies that didn't always move in synchronization completed activities right alongside extremely athletic bodies.

I will always remember the day I watched Sean, my middle son, run backward in front of a young boy in a wheelchair, helping him support a soccer ball on a bright orange cone he held in his hand. His caretaker maneuvered the wheelchair through the obstacle course Sean had set up. I will never forget those huge wide-open eyes and the smiles of the boys and girls from the special needs centers, as Tyler, my youngest son, handed them each their own Nike jersey and ball to take home.

During the summer of 2016 Josh returned to the Land of Bali. Packed in his suitcases were forty balls, soccer ladders, bibs, jerseys, and cones. This time half the forty children were special needs and the other half were scholarship students and children attending a private camp on the island. What an amazing integration of children all through the sport of soccer.

How rewarding it was watching children who had never interacted with someone in a wheelchair guide them through activities as a soccer buddy that day. How inspired we all were at the end of the day when all the children and their staff sang a song of friendship and gratefulness to coach Josh.

I am a very proud mother of three amazing sons.

Road to Wings

IT WAS TIME TO MAKE the next big decision on my journey. I had taken nearly two years off from working for an organization. I had used my creative abilities to expand, to become BIGGER! My savings had gone further than I anticipated, but now it was time to help locally and build up the means to continue on this journey of mine.

I had been asked to visit a school in the South Bay Area, one I had encountered during my six years at Oak Hill School. As a matter of fact, the founder of this South Bay school had come to Oak Hill a few years back asking for my help in completing the school's CDE (California Department of Education) certification packet.

Wings Learning Center had been founded by one mother whose son's educational choices were severely restricted. Aaron's mother persevered and established a school for him in Half Moon Bay, then moved it to San Mateo and finally to a two-story office building in Redwood City, where it supported about twenty students. The school had recently gone through some pretty tough times and was in need of someone to help put it back on its mission.

I was immediately hooked, first by the students, then by the passionate faculty and staff, and finally by the board's commitment to supporting the next leader in getting the school back on its meaningful journey.

The school was located over fifty miles from my home. To help out, I would have to cross the Golden Gate Bridge, travel bumper to bumper down 19th Avenue, get on Highway 280, then Route 92, and finally Highway 101 south before arriving at the doors of the school. What could I have been thinking when I said yes? I believe I was thinking that I could do this for a year, assess the challenges, develop an action plan and implement systems, and prepare the school for its long-term director. Well, as I write this section of the book, you need to know that I had just celebrated my seventh year at the school. So much for one year.

I was the new kid on the block, just handed a set of goals that were sure to make me a really big hit with the faculty. I had to cut $100,000 from the budget, meet with all the families to understand how they were feeling after some program challenges, help build their trust again, and evaluate why school districts were less than supportive of placing students.

I sent a letter to all district special education directors, inviting them to come meet with me and discuss their feelings, good, bad, or indifferent. I contacted parents and set a time to meet with them, and I scheduled a night to attend the parent meeting to field any questions families wanted to ask me in a group venue. Through these meetings, I gained insight into the fears, anxieties, and concerns of the families and districts. I developed a viable plan to address each concern.

Finally, I reviewed the budget and cut one full-time position, adjusted some overloaded salaries, instituted a benefit program to which staff would now have to contribute, and switched insurance coverage to a company I had done business with since Oak Hill School. All these adjustments helped to achieve the $100K cut, but they did not win me a great deal of trust with my new team.

I met with all the staff to find out how they were feeling about the recent school challenges before my first day of work and then for the next several months observed the program, attended meetings, facilitated IEP meetings, reviewed contracts, listened, and asked lots and lots of uncomfortable but necessary questions so I could come up with effective solutions.

The bottom line:

Wings Learning Center had a gift for helping children with autism communicate, learn independent living skills, access the community, and develop prevocational skills.

Wings Learning Center was filled with passionate faculty and staff who truly cared about the students and families.

The methodology that Wings Learning Center believed in was state of the art and, most important of all, effective and working with the students who attended.

The program had recently moved to a new building that needed some environmental changes; program policies needed to be tweaked; and a center needed to be opened for the entire education community to come view.

New boundaries needed to be established between staff, staff and families, and staff and the districts; a parent handbook created; and an employee handbook updated. Also needed was an admission process that would allow year-round placements and a consistent way of training each new staff or faculty.

New leaders needed to be developed within the current staff by increasing their knowledge and awareness of how effective schools are run.

Administrative faculty needed to understand the CDE system of certification, what the budget looked like, how it was developed, the education code behind the individual education planning meetings, and what district and special education local plan contracts contained.

Knowledge and transparency were key so faculty could understand why important changes needed to be made. Then Wings could take its much deserved place on the list of effective school programs for children with autism.

Over time the faculty, staff, and families grew to trust me and understand why I asked so many questions. They also began to accept my suggestions. Wings started to become a recognized program among families, districts, lawyers, and outside consultants. Its first three-year evaluation with the CDE, which I led, went well without any citations.

Over time the faculty grew from twenty to thirty to currently forty-four members. The number of classrooms grew from four to five and now six. Today's program serves forty children ages six to twenty-two in an amazing 18,000-square-foot remodeled building, with a great space for a sensory processing gym, rooms for three speech and language therapists to pull out or provide group sessions, a kitchen to teach cooking skills, a music therapy room to develop talent, space for us to deliver autism lectures to the community, space for yoga, and a large outside recess area where students could ride their scooters and bikes.

But I remember the times my business coordinator and I worried how we were going to meet payroll. I remember her staying in constant contact with district business offices, making sure they paid on time. Sometimes to save a week, she traveled to the district offices to pick up the check. I remember wondering which board member I would be asking for a temporary loan to meet payroll. I also remember the times we weren't sure teachers would last, whether we would have enough instructional assistants to provide the much-needed individualization, or if we would be able to find speech therapists and occupational therapists who truly understood how to develop appropriate relationships with our students, develop effective goals, and articulate their position at the often-intensive individual education planning meetings with parents and districts.

There were passionate professionals working at Wings. There was an amazing board of directors to support the mission and vision. There were talented therapists and teachers whose wisdom helped the children grow and learn, and there were many families who helped the school reach its goals each year.

The passionate teachers developed meaningful lessons to expand students' hygiene, dressing, toileting, reading, writing, cooking, and social skills.

The wise therapists addressed the students' limited receptive and expressive communication skills through creative sessions as well as their fine motor, motor planning, and sensory challenges through meaningful activities.

The board of directors provided their wisdom on financial challenges, and the families provided their gratitude through celebrations, donations, and notes of thankfulness.

The committed instructional assistants sat next to, walked with, and physically guided the students minute by minute, day by day, until each student gained more independence.

The faculty and staff changed soiled underwear, cleaned up spilled snacks and lunch items, assisted hand washing and nose blowing, and worked to maintain a safe and engaging environment for each student to learn.

In *The Wizard of Oz*, Dorothy, the Scarecrow, the Tin Man, and the Cowardly Lion rode through the Emerald City in a carriage led by the horse of many colors. Like that horse, who engaged all who set their eyes upon him, the team at Wings employed many eye-catching and creative activities and also collaborated together to provide a safe, caring, and structured environment for learning. Families felt that they could trust the Land of Wings and so they felt a sense of home for their children and themselves.

Karen Kaplan

Laxmi in the Land of Wings

WHEN I ARRIVED AT WINGS Learning Center, I was profoundly lucky to find yet another bright, caring, and passionate young woman who I believed had the skills to become a leader at the school and whom I learned to depend on.

Laxmi already possessed heart, and I felt that with more knowledge and more experience, she would be an amazing administrator by my side, helping Wings become all it could become.

Laxmi easily connected to each and every student who entered the school. She believed in their abilities. She could feel and understand their anxieties, and she always gave hope to the families by providing possible solutions and ideas.

She reminded me of myself in my younger years. We laughed, discussed, brainstormed, planned, and hoped together.

With Laxmi on staff, I finally reached a point when I felt that Wings would be in perfect hands on those days when I was unable to be on-site or when the time came for me to leave the school. This was much like when the Wizard of Oz took off in his hot-air balloon, leaving the Scarecrow to rule over the Emerald City.

I am proud and grateful for my relationship with this amazing young woman called Laxmi.

Lessons in the Land of Wings

THE FOLLOWING ARE SOME OF the lessons I have learned directing Wings Learning Center.

- There is implied power when you assume the head position at a school, and whether or not you think you have given everyone the feeling that you are approachable, they do not believe it.

- Listen, listen, listen. Did I say listen?

- Provide knowledge so that solutions are understood, thus implemented.

- There is no way you can please everyone so forgive yourself. It's okay to say no.

- Tough decisions have to be made by not-so-tough people.

- Make sure everyone feels appreciated and valued.

- Accept that change is inevitable.

- Realize that change brings new opportunities, and while it may not seem so at the start, it does.

- People will make mistakes; it is not the end of the world.

- People will not always like you or choose to be a friend, but striving for their respect is more important.

- Maintain a sense of humor at all times.

- Don't take things so personally (this one is really hard).

- Provide every possible, feasible resource to your team.

- Lead with brains, heart, courage, and a bit of wonder!

Other Stops on the Yellow Brick Road

I REMEMBERED THAT L. FRANK BAUM wrote many other books in the Oz series and that Dorothy traveled many times to Oz, exploring other parts beyond the Emerald City.

I, too, found myself exploring different projects on my Yellow Brick Road.

One day in 2008, I stood in front of fifty guests (families and professionals), facilitating a community gathering focused on what resources Marin currently offered and what needs the county had in supporting children with autism and their families. Hands raised and voices spoke out as I wrote what was needed on large pieces of paper: 1) more teachers trained, 2) more after-school opportunities, 3) better assessment, 4) more resources, 5) more in-home help, 6) more doctors who understand, (7) better outreach to the Hispanic community, and (8) more consistent programming across districts and more.

Then one mother stood up and asked, "Why is it that people in this community hide resources or just don't share resources with each other? Why is it that we all have to go so far away to obtain current state-of-the-art information to help our children?" I took a deep breath, pausing and processing her question in my head. I had what I thought a great answer, but one I was not going to share publically. Instead, I suggested that people in our community seem overwhelmed and lead such complex lives that perhaps there just isn't enough time. What I truly thought was that resources were so scarce and that families were so afraid of losing their appointment spots that they kept quiet. I also wondered why people had to travel so far to conferences and pay such high prices to obtain information.

My brain told me that it was possible to bring resources and information to our county, my heart believed in the need, and my courage said,

"Give it a try, Karen."

I had been in the autism field for over thirty years. How difficult could it be to put together a series of seven lectures each year that would bring meaningful information on autism to the San Francisco North Bay Area, to help administrators, teachers, therapists, mothers, fathers, grandparents, or medical practitioners? My father taught me the first important step. Never be afraid to ask for what you need. So I asked some of the leading experts and researchers I had met through the years: Emily Rubin, developer of the SCERTS Model; Michelle Garcia Winner, founder of Social Thinking; Dr. Robert Hendren, director of the MIND Institute; Dr. Bryna Siegel, author, researcher, and clinician at University of California, San Francisco; Dr. Lisa Croen, researcher at Kaiser Center for Autism; Dr. Grace Gengoux, psychologist and researcher from Stanford University; and Dr. Clifford Saron, researcher at the MIND Institute and father of a young man on the spectrum. They all said, "YES, of course Karen." The Marin Autism Lecture Series was then founded.

For each of the seven years that I offered the series, I took the first step, the ask, until I had offered nearly fifty lectures given by music therapists, creative arts therapists, speech therapists, occupational therapists, physical therapists, mothers, fathers, grandparents, scientists, doctors, researchers, and authors. The last lecture in the series, "Hear Our Voices," showcased the stories of those who lived each day on the spectrum. My guests heard the challenges of growing up on the spectrum, the strengths and gifts and talents of those with autism, and their hopes and dreams.

It was this final lecture series that moved me the most. To hear the unfair struggles of these young people, the lack of understanding by others, their need to isolate themselves, the limitations that society continues to place on them, and their hopes and dreams, much like those of any young person, brought me, as well as those guests in the room, to tears. I also felt some amazing giggles and "aha moments" in my heart that day.

The first lectures were held at the San Rafael Community Center. Then I found the best home for the series, Marin County Office of Education Conference Center. Thanks to the director of Special Education and the superintendent of schools, the site was offered free of charge. I was grateful. Once again the wisdom of my dad worked. I just asked. My hopeful intentions were heard.

The series was able to pay its speakers and provide scholarship for parents and teachers unable to afford the $25 lecture fee through donations from individuals, schools, and organizations that once again I had the courage to ask. I will always be grateful to Wells Fargo Bank, the Massocca family, Dr. Richard Orken and his wife, Cypress School, and Oak Hill School. They never missed a year with their support. Others also helped along the way: ANOVA School, Psychology Learning & You, Gateway Learning Group, and The Ryder Foundation, all of which invested in supporting children with autism and their families.

The Wizard of Oz was so very right. With brains, we can think and thus problem-solve as the Scarecrow learned he could do. It was the resource of knowledge I wanted to provide, giving hope that teachers, therapists, and most of all families would then find solutions to better support the understanding and growth of their children. It was hope I wanted to bring, so that no one else saw only despair and chose a path like ending a life.

I had learned that once mothers and fathers finally got their child with autism into bed, their next goal was to turn on their computers and begin the endless search for services and interventions.

There was no local venue that brought vendors and service providers together in the same room on one day for parents and professionals to access. So, why not me? I had been successful at developing the Lecture Series, why not a North Bay Autism Resource Fair, too?

Fifty tables first lined the gym at Dominican University of California in San Rafael and then the conference center at the Marin County Office of Education. So many groups and organizations were represented: schools, universities, therapy centers, parent support networks, the California Department of Rehabilitation, recreational centers, camps, bookstores, music therapists, speech therapists, behavior specialists, horseback-riding programs, respite care centers, and vocational and residential centers. The centers set up posters and put out brochures and sign-in sheets, connecting first with other resource centers, and then with the families that strolled through the fair.

That day, I was proud. That day, I thought, now a mother no longer has to stand up and say, "Services are not being shared within the community." I put together a program sheet listing all resources and made sure everyone who came through the doors of the fair took the sheet home.

But in 2015 there came the day when I could see that sharing resources in this format was no longer the most effective method, and so in 2016 I connected with the developer of another annual resource fair at Dominican University of California. This resource fair served families of typical children. I suggested that my community of special needs service providers set up information tables at the developer's one-day fair. My nonprofit made a donation to offset the costs of entrance fees, and my special needs service providers were invited to join. It gave me great satisfaction to know that special needs resource tables would finally sit side by side with the resource tables for typical children.

Hear Our Voices

FOR SIX YEARS, I HAD facilitated an autism lecture series in Marin County at the Marin County Office of Education in San Rafael, California. Hear Our Voices was my seventh and last lecture series. It ran from September 2015 until June 2016. I longed to provide an opportunity for parents and professionals to hear the words of those who lived each day on the autism spectrum.

Seven different panels of teens and adults living each day on the spectrum. Panelists with autism and Asperger sharing their lives with parents, grandparents, teachers, therapists, and counselors. Twenty different voices for us to listen to and learn from. Most could answer in phrases and sentences. Some needed to read from their notes. A few smiled, stated their names and where they attended school, and then showed us their gifts through a video or musical demonstration.

Some were in regular classrooms in the public schools. Some had additional support; others were in a special day class on a regular school site. Most were in private schools or had graduated from private schools after trying their best on local public school campuses. Several were attending college classes; others had graduated or left college.

I had drafted a set of questions and forwarded them to the panelists so that they would have time to process and reduce any question anxiety. Some were supported by their teachers or counselors as they prepared their responses. Most I met with beforehand to describe the environment they would be speaking in and to allow them to get to know me a little before the event.

In preparation, I made sure that lights were soft, water bottles available, and snacks present, and that panelists knew they could pass to someone else on any question. I made sure I explained to my panelists that we didn't always start on time because of traffic and parking. When the program began, I explained to the guests that we were not in a hurry and that questions might need to be repeated, passed on, and perhaps even restarted if the panelist lost his or her train of thought. The prompts and questions included these:

Tell us about yourself.

What are your interests, likes, hobbies, and talents?

Tells us about your social life (friends, family, and activities).

Tells us about your early years of school, middle years, and secondary years.

Who supported you through school?

What frustrations do you experience now?

What advice would you give parents and teachers to help them support those who live on the spectrum?

What hopes and dreams do you have for your future?

Here are some of their responses:

Tamsin

Just because you do not see the disability doesn't mean it's not there. Learn when to step in.

Be clear with us.

Be patient.

Vicki

I thank the teachers for teaching me how to be a better me.

Paul

Movement regulates me and helps me to be calm. I just couldn't process fast enough and didn't know how to organize.

I was bullied, held back twice, and then kicked out of class.

Mom placed me in a private adventure-based school and that truly helped me.

Greg

I am grateful that I liked women and was able to observe them to determine the social structure and ground rules.

Zen structure taught me how to observe.

When I was younger, being autistic felt like: being very lonely, being an alien species on a strange planet, being behind glass, being parachuted behind enemy lines and hoping the locals don't discover I am not one of them.

Presume competence.

Prepare children for the social world.

Luke

I want to own my own business.

I want to learn to drive a car.

(*to his parents*) Try to understand my emotions. Listen to me.

(*to his teachers*) Don't be too firm, be flexible. Have fun in class while teaching and be silly, too.

Matthew

I tried to fit in but didn't ever feel accepted. I'm pretty much a loner.

I finally found friends in an after-school game room.

(*to his teachers*) Take time, ask, and have an open mind.

I learned social skills from taking training in customer service.

When I am down I think, "Why was I born with this curse? Why am I the one left behind in friendships? Will I always be the background character, not able to take center stage?" But I am not a fan of drama. So, I don't really think of it. If someone is down, I try to help them out regardless of myself. If selfless is a trait, then that's what I am.

Stacey

I came out screaming.

I needed tutoring.

I had a tough father.

My mom was the breadwinner and taught me to speak up.

There were many lessons learned from this special lecture series. Here is one parent's insight:

> *As a parent to an autistic young adult, I found this series was so insightful. I have learned to step back, allow more room for my son to grow independent of me. It's very challenging and often a painful journey of letting go, as my desire is to surround and protect on every level. The bravery for all the panelists to speak their truth in front of an audience was inspiring.*
>
> —Janet Held, parent

Where Were We?

REMEMBER, IN THE VERY BEGINNING of my story, I mentioned that I was angered and frustrated after reading the chapter on autism in the book *Far from the Tree*, by Andrew Solomon? Well, I will confess that four years earlier, I read about a mother who shot her son and then herself. That very night I wrote what resembled a poem or maybe just a stream of consciousness, entitled "Where Were We?," to express the sadness that I felt in my heart and the words that kept announcing their presence in my head.

I Shot My Son with Autism and Then I Shot Myself

How did we fail this mother?

How did we fail this mother?

HOW DID WE FAIL THIS MOTHER?

Where were we when she reached out for guidance?

When she requested,

When she asked,

When she searched,

When she pleaded,

When she hoped and perhaps prayed for just one solution,

WHY DID WE NOT SEE

Her frustration,

Her anguish,

Her desperation,

Her pain,

Her hopelessness?

I paused and I thought, "This is 2012, everyone." And I screamed out, "Hello!"

We have acronyms for every governmental educational piece of law put into action: IDEA (Individuals with Disabilities Education Act), ISP (individual service plan), IEP (individual education plan), ITP (individual transition plan), IPP (individual program plan), FAPE (free appropriate public education), and 504 plans (the section of the Rehabilitation Act/Americans with Disabilities Act). We have Workability Services, Department of Rehabilitation Services, Regional Centers, and a Department of Developmental Services—all to help parents.

We have millions of website addresses focused on autism resources, training, and information for families to access. We have the California State Select Committee on ASD (autism spectrum disorder) to help parents.

We have family support groups like the Autism Society of America, Autism Speaks, Parents Helping Parents, Matrix Parent Network, FEAT (Families for Early Autism Treatment), TACA (Talk about Curing Autism), Support for Families, and more, so families can connect and not feel isolated.

We have a plethora of specialists (marriage and family therapists, behavior specialists, speech and language therapists, occupational therapists, physical therapists, education specialists, neurologists, and psychologists), all claiming to understand and support the needs of families.

So where were we when this mother saw no other choice but to take her son's life and her own?

Back to that poem in my head:

> Where were we?
>
> Did we not listen to her story, her needs?
>
> Did we not see her anguish, her fear?
>
> Did we not feel her hopelessness?
>
> Did we offer her anything?
>
> Should we have done something different?
>
> I KNOW I WILL TRY HARDER

If I Were a Parent

WHAT WOULD I DO IF I were a parent of a child with special needs?

How might I avoid reaching the very state this mother reached?

Where would I start?

I would take just two seconds, each day, before anyone woke, to light a small candle or stick of incense and ask for the ability to be grateful, patient, wise, and forgiving.

Next I would find a group of SISTERS who shared this different adventure I was now on and become an active participant in the group.

I would find every way to become knowledgeable about my child's strengths and challenges, so I could collaborate with the education and medical communities that offer interventions.

I would remember each day to accept my child for who he or she is and not what I hope he or she might become.

I would work very hard on giving myself permission, probably every day, maybe several times a day, not to feel I must have all the answers at once, do everything at once, and be everything to everyone (husband, child, siblings, parents, neighbors).

I would find every way I know how to make sure I got enough sleep every night.

I would have the courage to reach out to my friends and close family and explain to them who my child is and how I am feeling. I would explain to them how very important they will be in my life as I move through this path and how I hope they will be available to me.

I would find a counselor who could understand my feelings of sadness, loss, and being overwhelmed and set up regular sessions; maybe the counselor would specialize in loss, because I feel that before the birth of a child, we set expectations about the future with our child. We expect to see our child, with ten toes, ten fingers, and soft pink skin, develop mentally, physically, and emotionally perfect. When this does not happen and our dreams for this new being and ourselves cannot be realized, there is a loss.

I would follow the suggestions of Temple Grandin's mother and work really hard at giving myself permission to develop my own interests and take care of my own needs. I would work with my spouse or partner and try to develop a plan where we each have time to develop individually. If there were other children to consider, I would give myself permission to give them one-on-one time to meet their needs. If I thought a sibling group or counselor was needed, I would explore that as well.

I would develop a group of babysitters and allow myself time to have a real relationship with my significant other. Yes, I would also understand if occasionally we had to cancel our date together, but I would continue to try, not give up finding time to share moments in each other's embrace or company.

I would connect with financial planners who specialized in special needs financial planning and trusts and begin step-by-step to plan for my child's future. I would develop a three- to five-year plan and revisit it frequently to prepare for each stage of my child's life. The IEP (individual education plan) used in schools is a yearly evaluation plan, but I know that it is truly important to keep an eye on the future as well. It would be very late to begin to think about transition planning when my child reaches the age of sixteen. I would think about the future and evaluate it yearly, but I would find a way to keep my eyes on the larger picture.

I know there has got be an overwhelming feeling of desperation when parents realize their child will be living beyond their time. "Who will watch over our child as I do?" they must think. "Who will make sure our child's life is lived well?" they must wonder. Taking the time now to create a team of caring family, friends, and colleagues who can offer their guidance when parents are no longer able could provide peace of mind in this area. Parents can contact legal advisors who can help them design this plan right now.

Books written by parents can be helpful in getting through this new adventure that I am now on. These books offer great advice from those who have come before me. I would read some of these as well as connect with reliable website articles and blogs. I would attend seminars, conferences, and workshops put on by experienced and knowledgeable parents and professionals. I would find ones that resonate with my adventure each year. Connecting with others I might feel less isolated.

I would learn to become my child's best advocate. I have seen parents who are well versed in their child's strengths and challenges, those who understand how the systems work, and those who can calmly, professionally, and collaboratively communicate with education, medical, and therapeutic communities. They are the ones who will receive the services. I would learn all the basic rules and then I would learn every possible strategy for playing the game to win.

If I had become a parent of a child with special needs, my life would surely have been different. But my life would still have been formed by the choices I made along the way and it would have been affected by the opportunities that showed up on my path. I know that I, too, would have felt a loss, but I also know I would have tried to do my very best as I know those parents with a special needs child are doing. I hope with the ideas I have mentioned, a mother might be less likely to feel so isolated, so depressed, or so without choices that she sees no solution other than to shoot her child and herself.

I am the mother of three young men, and my life is different because of them. I feel I have done the best I could with the choices I made and the opportunities that came along on this adventure with them. I still light my stick of incense each morning and identify what I am grateful for as well as ask for guidance in making wise decisions. I still work continually on letting go of anything that does not serve me in a positive way, and I still work each and every day on being patient. The work is never done. I do, by the way, ask for prosperity, and sometimes I play Mega Millions and SuperLotto to help with the journey.

I realize that I do not have the added challenges and feelings of loss that parents with special needs children have, and in no way do I want to make light of their complex lives. I just want mothers to see that there are choices, opportunities, and help for both themselves and their children. I do hope that they can see their son's or daughter's special gifts and talents, as I would try to see them, and not be in so much pain to choose the solution the mother above chose.

There may be no Land of Oz, filled with witches and wizards who can grant wishes, but there are friends, family, SISTERS of the same kind, and teachers like me whom you can reach out to for help and support.

No Way, Dr. Bettelheim

It was late 1980, and I was on my way to a hotel located close to the San Francisco Airport, in Burlingame. I was off to see a man named Bruno Bettelheim, who was the first to blame mothers of children with autism and likened the child's experiences to those left in concentration camps.

Since my college days at Arizona State University, I had been deeply involved with families, getting to know their frustrations, anxieties, questions, hopes, fears, and dreams for their sons and daughters. I can say without hesitation that I have never met the "refrigerator mom" whom Dr. Bruno Bettelheim wrote about.

The term "refrigerator mother" was coined in the 1940s as a label for mothers of autistic children. These mothers were blamed for their children's autism. As a result, mothers of children with autism suffered from blame, guilt, and self-doubt from the 1950s throughout the 1970s and beyond.

After scientists had first described the symptoms, and in the absence of any known biomedical causes of autism, leading psychoanalyst Bruno Bettelheim, a University of Chicago professor and child development specialist, championed the notion that autism was the product of mothers who were cold, distant, and rejecting, thus depriving babies of the chance to bond properly. The theory was embraced by the medical establishment and went largely unchallenged into the mid-1960s, but its effects have lingered into the twenty-first century.

I had read Bettelheim's book *The Empty Fortress* but couldn't believe its conclusions. I had met those so-called refrigerator mothers and heard their stories about their son or daughter who never seemed to care if they were in the room or not, who did not enjoy peekaboo or lift their arms to be picked up from their crib. I had heard their stories of trying to comfort their young children during sleepless nights, and their crying spells, and how they longed to be hugged back. I had never heard any stories of any child lacking stimulation, safety, food, or water or experiencing isolation like those in concentration camps. I had not met one cold and uncaring refrigerator mother or father, but only parents who would do anything to help their child. I had seen desperation, sometimes loss of hope, sometimes fear, and of course anxiety from not knowing what to do, whom to turn to, or where to go for help.

I definitely had to meet this Dr. Bettelheim and understand why he was considered knowledgeable in this field of autism. Perhaps I had something to learn from him.

I sat in the audience, maybe with a hundred other guests, waiting to hear his wisdom, and watched as a small, elderly man, a bit hunched over, walked through the middle aisle of the assembly-style chairs.

He was introduced and all his education and degrees were noted. He spoke a bit about traditional education and what was lacking, and then it began: pontification on his professional research and conclusions about autism. I don't remember all the details that sputtered out of his mouth, but I do remember the sentence that stimulated me to raise my hand and explore. He said that if mothers had only breast-fed their children with autism, autism would never have occurred.

Really, it was as easy as that. Wow. Up went my hand. "Yes, Madame, what is your question?"

I stood up and let the doctor know that I was a bit confused. I offered the simple fact that my mother never breast-fed me, and I had no diagnosis of autism.

The lecturing began.

"You probably have little or no experience in autism. What degrees do you possess? You probably haven't even seen children with autism," the Doctor announced.

"Dr. Bettelheim, I am a licensed speech pathologist and also hold my teaching credential in the area of several handicaps. I also have been working with children with autism since 1971."

Again, that small, elderly man, so honored for his knowledge, said, "You probably are not seeing children with autism and you do not have the experience and degrees you would need to know."

I sat down quietly and that day realized this man, who had created so much hurt, so much misunderstanding about these children and their families, had little to offer me on my journey. At the break, I left.

In 1964, Bernard Rimland, a psychologist with an autistic son, published a book that signaled the emergence of a counter-explanation to the established misconceptions about the causes of autism. His book *Infantile Autism: The Syndrome and Its Implications for a Neural Theory of Behavior* attacked the refrigerator mother hypothesis directly.

Bettelheim was considered a leading authority on autism until his death, when it was revealed that he had plagiarized others' work and falsified his credentials.

I am so happy I left at the break that day.

Articles for Families

I HAVE ALWAYS BELIEVED THAT parents are key to the success of their child's education, emotional well-being, and independence.

I have witnessed how their hearts, courage, and knowledge lead them to establish schools, centers, vocational opportunities, and living communities; bring awareness to communities; change laws; and establish new policy. I have seen parents start associations, establish foundations, and fill the publishing houses with stories of sadness, frustration, hope, impossible journeys, and successes.

I applauded their commitment and passion to help others as they helped their own son or daughter.

During my forty years supporting children and families, I have also felt conflicted, frustrated, disappointed, and saddened by the actions of some. I took to writing a series of articles (see articles by Karen Kaplan at specialneeds.com) for one year, hoping to lead parents away from their feelings of guilt, entitlement, anger, and nonacceptance. I wanted them to think about how they might be overprotecting their children or underestimating what their children were capable of. I wanted them to see possibilities and opportunities.

My article "Firing the Butler and the Maid" provided an opportunity to discuss some of the things that seem to hold parents hostage, keeping them from planning ways to help their son or daughter develop independence. First, there is guilt that they caused the disability, then their lack of time due to the complex needs of the family, and then the fact that they are unaware of where to begin helping their child or are thinking their child can't possibly do the task correctly.

I hoped that my suggestions might give these parents some ideas of where to start, how to start, and why they needed to start helping their children solve their own problems, participate in chores, initiate, request before obtaining, and make an independent choice instead of being given what the parents think the children need.

I reminded parents that each time they expect their children to initiate, make a request, respond to a question, or find a solution, they would be increasing cognitive development. I gave them a list of little tasks they could begin to teach their sons or daughters:

Unload the silverware tray in the dishwasher.

Carry the laundry basket from their room to the laundry room.

Carry an item or two from the grocery store trip into the house and put it away.

Carry their own backpack into school.

Choose the top they will wear to school (give a choice of two).

Request a jar, box, or package to be opened before you open it.

Choose between weekend activities (park, movies, walk, etc.).

Turn the correct knobs on the bathtub, shower, sink, washer, and dryer.

Put one or two items on the meal table.

Pick up after themselves, put toys away, and hang up their own jacket.

I explained that it wasn't necessary for the child to complete the whole task or to do the task perfectly or every day, especially during the school week. The child could instead start on a Saturday or Sunday. In other words, I was asking mothers and fathers to fire themselves as maids and butlers early on in their child's life and rehire themselves as coaches, teaching essential skills to prepare their child for the game of life.

I wanted parents to believe that their children are capable and can learn when they are expected to, and accept when their child is not successful right away and be patient. I wanted parents to know that their son or daughter may take much longer to learn tasks of daily living, so it was critical that they start early. I wanted them to be hopeful.

"Getting Out of Our Own Way," Rescue Less," and "Parents as Partners" spoke to parents who drop their son or daughter off at the school's front door or place their child on the yellow school bus each day, uttering

"Have a great day" and expecting the school team to prepare their child for life. These are the parents who attend the yearly IEP meeting and promise to have their son or daughter start chores at home but never follow through.

Again, I understood that cultural beliefs and values, lack of time, wanting to avoid confrontation, or an inability of accept imperfection may get in the way of parents starting. But I also knew that schools are not entirely responsible for preparing the child for life.

When I decided to have children, I remember thinking, "This is a huge responsibility and my needs will just have to take a backseat." With each of my three sons' births, I realized that their health, their education, and their social life would take precedence over my own, and that I would have to find a way to adjust. I knew I would have to make plans as well to find help along the way.

I kept in mind that the pain and guilt these parents experienced could be deep if they were unable say no to their son or daughter. I kept in mind how isolated they must be to allow their child to be in control, instead of setting rules and boundaries.

I tried to help them understand that the longer they waited, the more dependent their child would become, the more resistant their child would be to changing habits, and the more likely their child's adult living, working, and recreation options would be reduced, restricted, and limited.

I urged parents to first forgive themselves and pleaded with them to find a way to let go of preconceived negative ideas: my children will never learn, or it's just too early, my child won't do it, or I don't have time to do it, it's the school's responsibility, or the occupational therapist or speech therapist will take care of it, or I can't learn how to help.

I asked that parents develop an attitude of possibility thinking, as Dr. Robert Schuller recommends, and create a plan, just as Dorothy, the Scarecrow, the Tin Man, and the Cowardly Lion did, to accomplish their goals. Parents needed to remember that their child's education did not stop when the bus came to pick them up for school, or when it dropped them back home.

Old, culturally based beliefs may have to be altered. Parents may need to know that they are still good parents even if they stop doing everything for their son and begin to facilitate independence. The caretaker role needs to change to care-teacher role.

Families who hire in-home help for their children need to ensure that care providers are not doing everything for their children but instead are encouraging them to develop independence.

I advised parents to implement some of the following practices as early as possible:

Take their children to a variety of events, remembering the parents do not have to stay the length of the event

Teach "No," "Wait," "Not now," "First this, then that"

Encourage them to share the front seat and backseat with their sibling

Facilitate greeting others

Model pushing the shopping cart in Safeway

Praise putting their toys back

Request that they get their own jacket and lunch bag when it is time to go to school

Encourage a few steps of all hygiene tasks

Have them complete a chore at home to develop a sense of family contribution

Unfortunately, I still see some families continuing to carry their sixteen-year-old son's backpack and lunch bag to school, shop for and prepare all his meals, and meet all his laundry needs, yet somehow expect him to live in an apartment and find something meaningful to do in his life.

I believe parents have to find a balance between leading with their hearts and having the courage to lead with the knowledge they obtain along the way. They may have to adjust along the road, as new challenges arrive and new goals have to be met, in order to find their way home.

I believe the Wizard of Oz would say to these parents, "Throw away the blame card, let go of your guilt, become a coach, take small manageable steps toward helping your son or daughter develop patience, respect, and responsibility, and reach out and seek help."

Secure Your Own Mask First

THE STORY OF THE MOTHER who shot her son is never far from my mind, so when I am designing workshops I try hard to include tips and strategies that will help families.

"In case of an emergency, secure your own mask before securing your child's." This is a statement we hear each time we fly anywhere in the world.

If mothers and fathers of children with special needs are going to feel hope and well-being, rather than isolation, fear, anxiety, or helplessness, they will need to develop their own life-mask strategies.

I have tried to send this message to families at the schools I direct, to the faculty and staff I supervise, and to the families and professionals in other cultures I have mentored.

In that process, I have used a variety of visual pictures, quotes, and stories that might help start a life-mask strategy.

"To keep a lamp burning, we have to put oil in it." Our bodies, minds, and souls are the lamp, and without fuel the lamp will not burn brightly and show the way, and our bodies, minds, and souls will not move us in the right direction.

Parents often experience sleepless nights or long evenings, cruising the Internet for interventions, facts, and research that may offer something to help their son or daughter. Their to-do or to-know lists are endless. Stress builds up as they wonder whether they will ever get everything done. They worry about the future. They worry about the now. They may lose concentration and begin to forget important things each day. They may overeat or under-eat, or have headaches. They have forgotten to put the oil in their lamp bodies that they need to fuel themselves.

I start by suggesting that they find some time in their day or night to take a walk, attend a yoga or exercise class, or join a gym. Then I encourage them to make a small amount of time to do something they enjoy, if not weekly, then monthly or every other month (art class, movie, theater, or concert). These activities are the oil they need to maintain a positive outlook and provide rest from the constant to-do lists and the worrying. If only for a short amount of time, parents can focus on the walk, the exercise, the movie, and perhaps find some relief.

To some, I suggest getting out in nature to enjoy the silence, if just for twenty or thirty minutes.

I tell them that I read that "laughter is inner jogging and that a hundred belly laughs are the cardiovascular equivalent of ten minutes of rowing." I suggest they schedule a time to watch a funny movie, go hear a comedian, or meet with girlfriends and guy friends and joke with each other.

I share with them a strategy I read about, where you write down everything that stresses you out. Then separate the list into things you can't control and those you can, and write down one step toward controlling the ones you can. Let go of the ones that are out of your control. I also tell them that it could help to write down one thing that was positive about their day each night.

One of the hardest pieces of advice for these parents to implement seems to be saying no and reducing, as much as possible, the number of people in their lives who drain them, those who have some negative impact on their lamp burning brightly. I tell them to engage with those who lighten and support their lives.

For both parents and professionals, I have quoted research studies from North Carolina State University, Michigan State University, University of Washington, Phil Jackson of the Los Angeles Lakers, and Silicon Valley technology companies all indicating that meditation and mindfulness training have proved effective in helping to decrease stress, increase positive emotions, and maintain better physical and mental health.

Taking time for a massage, new nail polish, perhaps a new haircut or hairdo, or even a new pair of shoes could help you feel more positive about yourself and could be especially helpful before a special meeting just like Dorothy's with the Wizard of Oz.

I like to share a story about geese with professionals and families who rely on each other for help and support at their schools, centers, or homes.

Once there was a kindergarten teacher who took her children outside when they became restless and lay down with them on the grass to watch the clouds. She made up stories for them while they watched. One day they watched a flock of geese fly by, honking. The children looked up and they made up names for the geese with their teacher. The teacher's husband encouraged her to study geese so she could make up informative stories about geese for her students. Here are the lessons she taught her children:

Each bird in the V formation creates uplift to keep the birds flying. Together the flock creates 71 percent more uplift by staying together, which keeps the flock flying longer.
Lesson 1: Work collaboratively; share a common direction.

When one bird gets tired, it falls back in the V formation to take advantage of the lift from others.
Lesson 2: Accept help from others who have a similar vision for they will help us as well.

When the lead goose gets tired, the flock rotates the lead.
Lesson 3: Take turns on hard tasks.

Geese are always honking because they are thanking the leader for flying so fast and strong.
Lesson 4: It is important for us to encourage others for jobs well done.

When a goose gets sick, wounded, or shot, two others drop off to each side of the ailing goose and take it to the ground to protect it. They stay until the goose is well or dies.
Lesson 5: Stand by each other in difficult times as well as when you are all strong.

I read another book years ago that resonated with me: *Out of Apples*, by Lee Schnebly, a certified mental health counselor. Her metaphor that each of us has, and must maintain, an apple barrel is a helpful reminder to parents of special needs children—and those professionals who work with them—to take care of their own well-being and make sure they don't give all their apples away; otherwise, they risk falling deep into a depression or, worse, taking the life of their child or their own.

Lee reminds us that our life's activities fill our barrel and also deplete our barrel. She reminds us that many types of apples are available and that it is our responsibility to get whatever apples we want and keep our barrel full. Going to a favorite place, reading a favorite book, seeing our child learning, and spending time with close friends and with family give us apples we can add to our barrel. Listening to our favorite music, spending time alone, eating ice cream, and dancing are also great apples to add to our barrel.

On the other hand, being overworked, getting sick, arguing with a loved one, letting someone down, not being able to help everyone, and not making time to do any of our favorite things are ways that our apples are given away. Holding feelings in, not sharing the load, and being angry, anxious, or confused deplete the apples in our barrel.

For parents of a special needs child, attending a negative IEP with a school district, losing services, learning your child has had an incident at school, witnessing your child develop a seizure disorder during adolescence, or needing to consider medication for your child—all these represent an apple you have had to give away, depleting your apple barrel.

Parents and professionals, please keep an eye on your barrel's fullness. If the bottom is visible, stress increases and your emotional and physical well-being suffers. Check nightly on that barrel's fullness. Plan a way to refill the barrel as it gets low. Avoid getting to where you see the bottom over and over again. Please.

Tough Times Never Last, But Tough People Do!, by Dr. Robert Schuller, was another book I read very early on the Yellow Brick Road. Dr. Schuller had great wisdom that I have shared with parents and those I have mentored. Perhaps some of this wisdom could change a parent's decision made in desperation.

We have the choice to look at any situation and take it with a negative or positive attitude. Choose positive.

Look at what you have left, not what you have lost.

Keep your optimism growing by tapping into positive memories. Recall them, especially successes, and learn from them, as they can bring you power.

Don't make key decisions at a low point in your life.

Take small steps at first, but never lose sight of the end results you want.

Believe things are possible.

Seeing Gifts and Talents

ON APRIL 2, 2016, I DREAMED up Autism Awesomeness, an event that would occur each April during Autism Awareness month, to celebrate and bring hope. I thought again about how I might help parents to feel hopefulness, professionals to feel appreciated, and, most of all, those living on the autism spectrum to be seen as individuals who come into the world like all of us, with strengths, gifts, and talents.

It didn't sit so well with me to consider that during Autism Awareness month, I would again be inundated with questions from the media about the statistics of autism's growth, complaints of limited or nonexistent supports and services, stories of the tragedies parents have experienced, or reports on what the government wasn't doing enough of and what schools weren't doing at all.

It was not my intention to make light of the need for continued awareness, the need to inspire more teachers to understand and support their students with autism, the need to create more jobs and more living options, and the need to enable the medical and scientific communities to continue their search for effective interventions and strategies. But I wanted to create an event where everyone left with hope, not despair or anxiety.

All year long, I had listened to the voices of teens and adults who lived each day on the spectrum. I listened to the stories about their struggles, their dreams, and their hopes. Their hopes were absolutely no different from the hopes of my own sons.

Will, attending a special school for students with special needs, wanted to spend time socializing with his friends, live on his own in an apartment, travel, and play music.

Tamsin, currently taking classes at the junior college, wanted to move out of a supervised living environment, drive a car, advocate for others like herself, and work with children in a school setting.

Greg wanted to find a way to use all his amazing technical and mechanical skills to establish a profitable business.

Matthew wanted to be a successful DJ or the engineer behind the scenes on a radio station.

Paul hoped to cross-country ski across the Arctic, bringing awareness to the strengths of those on the spectrum.

Sophie wanted to do voice-overs.

Stacey wanted to perform on stage and be a successful singer in musical productions.

Jamie, who spoke fluent Japanese, wanted to learn how to become a buyer at a local retail store and work full time instead of short hours in an entry-level position.

John and Tosh, who joined each other for the first time on the stage, one playing guitar and the other drums at "Autism Awesomeness," wondered where their musical ability might take them.

Stacey and Matthew, a couple, wanted to move out of their parents' homes and find some way to finance living together so they could enjoy a typical man and woman relationship.

Rose wanted to find the perfect job testing and creating games for gaming companies like Nintendo®.

Anlor wanted to publish her memoir to bring awareness of the world of autism to people outside the spectrum.

Jonathan hoped to find someone special one day and get married.

Jasmine hoped to find a job, travel, and maybe take a class at the local junior college.

Their hopes were no different from those of others not challenged by autism. I don't think I know of a teen or young adult who doesn't want to find a special someone at some point, engage with a friend of like mind, perhaps seek postsecondary education, or identify a job aligned with interests and skill sets, enjoy the privacy of one's own living space, and find effective transportation.

I have started having conversations with the mothers and fathers, asking them to tell me their son's or daughter's interests. I help them understand that while it is important to work on communication expression and understanding, self-regulation, and all the skills of daily living with their children, the key is to make sure they develop their interests. Interests and curiosities are what help us to find purpose, meaning, and enjoyment in life. They lead us to our professions, where we find our friends or where we might volunteer.

When a mother gives me that vacant look, thinking, "My son doesn't really have any interests," I ask, "With whom is he the most happy? What activities make him smile and stay engaged? Where does he seem most content?" Then the look changes. "My son likes being at the movie theater." Another mom says her son likes being at the horse stables and a third says her son enjoys riding his bike.

Okay, we have a start. I say, think of all the jobs people do at the movie theater. Ticket taker, refreshment stand server, candy stocker, theater janitor are a few I come up with quickly. Let's teach your son to do all of them and then he can watch the movie for a job well done.

Riding stables may offer volunteer or job opportunities such as grooming, feeding, and maintaining barns and horse stalls. Taking a horse for a ride after a successful workday not only cheers up your son but also exercises the horse. Perhaps someday he might help at the riding stables.

Let's teach your son to wash his bike, change a tire, oil the chain, and polish the seat. Then he can ride his bike. Someday he might help out at a bike repair shop.

What Does the Fork in the Road Mean?

SOMETIMES EACH OF US REACHES a fork in our road. Dorothy had been following the Yellow Brick Road after leaving Munchkin Land and didn't know which way to choose. All of a sudden she heard, "That way is a nice way." Then, "It's pleasant that way, too." Finally, she hears, "Some people go both ways."

That is exactly what happened to me on my road with autism. I seemed to be traveling for a while, finding purpose in each turn I took. And then I'd come to a fork. Sometimes the fork represented the end to one way I had traveled, suggesting it was time to try a new direction. Sometimes the fork presented an impasse that cannot be broken through, so I had to leave and find another route.

Each time I evaluated which direction might be worthy of my time and then put my best foot forward. Sometimes I met people along the way who gave me additional information to help me move in the best direction.

For example, after seven years of putting on the lecture series, I realized I was at a fork in the road. The series would end in May of 2016. I just didn't have another series in me. I wasn't sure what road I might take next. Perhaps none. Then I saw an opportunity. I found a way to address my curiosities of long ago.

I decided that I would create a yearly day of hopefulness. The first year's conference on hopefulness would bring together professionals who could help parents understand how important it was to build as early as possible independent sons and daughters with special needs. The conference would be called Road to Independence and occur in the fall each year.

This idea was based on my earlier writings: "Firing the Butler and the Maid," "Rescue Less," and "Getting Out of Our Own Way." It was so timely to put on this type of conference.

Children with autism and other special needs were graduating from the supporting arms of school districts. Young adults with autism and other developmental learning challenges were finding out that they were unprepared to take on the jobs that were available, live on their own, or problem-solve without someone's 24/7 help. They found out that programs were not ready to support them. They realized their school programs had not prepared them. They found out, too late, that their parents should have encouraged them to build their independence earlier. They were now coming face to face with challenges at every turn.

So, on October 1, 2016, a one-day conference called Road to Independence presented ideas, strategies, self-help tips, research, and interventions on how to build independent young men and women. It showcased a panel of young adults sharing their stories about how difficult it is for them to live independently because they weren't prepared and then, through them, provided hope to families and those who strive to be independent.

I have no idea what each future conference will look like, but I will remember that it is only a simple fork in the road where I will stand, pause, breathe, and evaluate the possibilities of bringing something meaningful and hopeful to the families. I will know that a new adventure waits for me on my road with autism.

Saying Good-Bye to Bali for Now

"PLEASE LET'S NOT SAY GOOD-BYE, Ibu," said Yuni at our final dinner at the Bridges Restaurant in Ubud. Each year, she and Adi, her husband, one or more of my sons, and I would enjoy an amazing dinner and think about what we might accomplish the next summer, when I returned. "Let's just say, 'See you later.'" I agreed, then we hugged and she and Adi hopped into their car and drove back to the Denpasar area.

I am not exactly sure when I had the feeling that the summer of 2016 might be the last time I would travel to the island of Bali to teach for a while. I am also not sure when I began to think it was time for me to identify other in-need communities to learn from and to share what I knew.

Then it was June 23, 2016, the day of my last presentation at the Annika Linden Centre. I had been on the island since June 4 this time and had completed at least five other workshops for teachers, therapists, families, and staff. This workshop was designed to help teachers and administrators understand how to develop a vocational program for those with disabilities.

I was hoping to help everyone see these children as more capable, "not less than." I hoped they would begin to believe that those with special needs could be trained to do work and give back. The guests at the workshop shared that most people and businesses felt that people with disabilities were less than. They feared that programs developed to train these types of children and adults would displace workers who were typical. I suggested, then, that perhaps these children could start with just volunteering at businesses so that others could experience their capabilities.

I also suggested that the teachers and administrators might teach these children to do a wide variety of jobs at their own center sites. Staff could then film them and share actual proof of their abilities with those who did not believe. They smiled. I am not sure if the smiles meant agreement or if any of these alternative ideas would be implemented, but I left them there to consider.

I realized that day that acceptance truly required not only expanded knowledge but time. I knew that the knowledge (ideas, information, resources, and suggestions) I had brought to the island during my seven trips would now need time to be processed, understood, evaluated, and aligned in a culture very different from America. I knew it would also take much heart and courage from the Balinese in order to change current beliefs and attitudes so that those with disabilities on the island might find their way home.

The evening of my last workshop I sat down to write this stream of consciousness:

Good-Bye to Bali for a While

I have climbed the temples

I have walked the rice paddies

I have wrapped a sarong around my waist and prayed in gratitude

I have tasted red rice

I have sipped turmeric with lemon and honey

I have chewed coconut slices

I have sipped cashew milk in my coffee

I have felt the sting of the hot chile-pepper oil on my tongue

I have felt aloe vera, mango, and coffee scrubbings on my body and soaked in aromatic tubs with floating flower petals of purple, red, and pink

I have held on and leaned right and left on the back of motorbikes

I have sat and lain upon bolsters and yoga mats twisting, turning, stretching, lengthening, bending, and balancing, with eyes wide open and eyes closed shut, breathing deeply in and lengthening the exhale

I have walked through temples on mountains, temples in villages, temples on lakes, and temples in the sea

I have watched the large, black bull sarcophagus filled with bone travel through the streets supported by Gamelans playing and families ready to celebrate the soul's release of their loved one

I have observed workers, carvers, painters, designers, photographers, chefs, teachers, dancers, drummers

I have met physiotherapists, occupational therapists, speech therapists, psychologists, special teachers, and directors of NGOs

I have greeted children with autism, Down syndrome, attention deficit disorder, cerebral palsy, intellectual disability, and other complex genetic challenges

I have watched, listened, collaborated, questioned, and offered research, definitions, explanations, ideas, strategies, wisdoms, interventions, curriculums, activities, experience, hope, understanding, different perspectives, resources, and gratitude

I have seen my sons mentor, inspire, and give selflessly

I have seen typical children embrace their peers with unique differences on the soccer fields

I have discussed autism, Down syndrome, cerebral palsy, attention deficit disorder, self-help skill development, prevocational development, fundraising, behavior challenges, cooking curriculums, sensory integration, and communication challenges

My computer is filled with amazing megabytes of photos and words in Bahasa Indonesian to recall and express this journey

I will miss the colors, the ceremonies, and the wide-eyed compassion of those wanting to make a difference in the lives of those with special needs

I will miss the children so capable of more

But acceptance takes not only knowledge but heart and courage— and TIME

When I boarded EVA Air to return to California in July of 2016, I was already reflecting on the wisdom I had gained and the friendships I had made. I was truly curious about where the Yellow Brick Road might take me next.

Finding Purpose

My second favorite childhood film, *The Wizard of Oz,* is a story that not only helps me think about my purpose in life, helping those living with autism and special needs, but also helps me talk about my spiritual journey in this life.

The year that I assumed the position of director of Oak Hill School, I found Joey Green's book *The Zen of Oz: Ten Spiritual Lessons from Over the Rainbow,* first published in 1998, sitting on the bookshelf with other books on Buddhism at the Open Secret Book Store in San Rafael.

I smiled, maybe even giggled, and thought, "Got to read this one, for sure." I learned about Spirit Rock, a retreat center only twenty minutes from my house in San Anselmo, which offered workshops, events, and retreats for those looking to understand the principles of Buddhism. I planned to enroll in one or more of these activities. I was searching, trying to understand this road I was on with autism and life.

I was about to take my first yoga class. I had just completed reading a first book on the principles of Buddhism. Both the class and the book seemed to resonate with me. Now, I found myself standing in Open Secret, holding in my hands *The Zen of Oz,* which drew an analogy between the search for our purpose in life and Dorothy on the Yellow Brick Road. This was very interesting.

The author sees that the story of the Wizard of Oz can be about any one of us who is in search of his or her true self. Dorothy is trying to find her way back home. She is a seeker looking for purpose, acceptance, and love. Joey Green reminds the reader what Professor Marvel tells Dorothy in the film when she runs away from the farm—that she just can't run away from her problems but must confront them and take control of her own life choices. This is what Dorothy learns on the Yellow Brick Road.

The author explains that the path is not always easy. Dorothy experiences a tornado, talking trees throwing apples at her, a dark forest with "lions and tigers and bears," and near death by poppies. But by helping the Munchkins escape from the tyranny of the Wicked Witch of the West, freeing the Winkies and the Winged Monkeys, freeing the Wizard of Oz from ruling the Emerald City, and helping the Scarecrow, the Tin Man, and the Cowardly Lion find their place and purpose, she discovers her own.

I lost the Kaplan Foundation, a twenty-year marriage, and my mother and father along my path. But I have never given up. I tackled each problem presented in the best way I knew how. I helped others along the way find resources, solutions, knowledge, and their own power within.

"Never let go of those Ruby Red Slippers," says Glinda. "They must be very powerful." Joey Green feels that the Ruby Red Slippers represent our passions, our uniqueness, our individuality, our purpose. We must never give them up by taking them off. "Rubies are precious gemstones," he says. Our passion and purpose are also precious. I may have lost the feeling of the ruby shoes on my feet every now and then, but I never gave them up. I believe I have stayed true to my passion and purpose. Yes I have questioned my own uniqueness and capabilities along the way and I have paused at forks in my Yellow Brick Road, but I have taken those key steps forward in discovering my own power.

Joey Green writes that just as Dorothy discovered when she met the Scarecrow, the Tin Man, and the Cowardly Lion, we never travel alone on the road. I, too, was never truly alone. There were my father's words that always guided me and gave me courage. There were the children who led me and the families who had faith in me. There were my mentors who encouraged me, and there were my three sons, who were proud of me and reminded me how important it is to lead with the heart.

Joey Green emphasizes a statement the Wizard makes: "A heart is judged not by how much you love, but by how much you are loved by others." He adds, "Being loved by others is equal to how deeply we love ourselves as well." What he is saying, I believe, is we must have self-love and perform selfless acts of kindness. This is a Zen principle. When the Tin Man says, "I will get Dorothy to the Wizard of Oz whether or not I get a heart," he is demonstrating his selflessness.

Dorothy is always focused on the possibilities. She assures the companions she meets along the way that once they get to the Emerald City and meet the Wizard, all their heart's desires will be fulfilled. She visualizes positive outcomes all along the way.

I have always tried to see the glass half full. I practice visualizing positive outcomes. I have always borne in mind the spirit of Robert Schuller's principles of possibility thinking. I also listened to *The Little Engine That Could*, which my father first read to me and then I did over and over again. The little engine chugged over the mountain saying, "I think I can, I think I can," and he did, bringing the train-load of toys to children who would have never received any toys that year.

I have even thought about how the letters in Oz so closely match the letters in om, the sound chanted by many Buddhists and those who practice yoga. I looked up the meaning of om and learned that it is a mystical sound. And we all know that Oz was a mystical place for sure. We even think about the om sound creating a special state of mind for each of us. And we know Oz was a place Aunt Em thought was just a state of mind in Dorothy's head.

Today, I find home in restorative and Yin yoga. I find serenity in lighting my simple incense each morning and visualizing positive outcomes in my life and in the lives of others. I find peacefulness in thinking about what and whom I am grateful for in my life. Today, I still find myself thinking I can. I still find myself knowing my purpose is to teach and help others. I also find myself at forks on the Yellow Brick Road. But I am working on thinking, "Well, isn't that curious" instead of "lions and tigers and bears, oh my!"

The Search for Purpose or Finding Our Heart's Desire

FOR THOSE OF US WHO are searching for purpose in life, our heart's desire, the story of Dorothy in the Land of Oz may resonate. Dorothy dreams of being somewhere "Over the Rainbow" in that "land that we dream of," that special place we hope to reach, in our lives. But it isn't until Dorothy lands in the Land of Oz, after being hit over the head with a flying window in the tornado, that she discovers her true heart's desire is to be back in Kansas, with her family. Glinda the Good Witch tells Dorothy that she always possessed the power to return home, but she first had to find out what she truly wanted before she could use the Ruby Red Slippers to fulfill her desire. Perhaps Dorothy had taken for granted what her life offered back in Kansas, but as she took control of her journey in the Land of Oz and helped others find their way, she realized her own heart's desire was to return home. When she realizes this, she takes charge of her life, never giving up, and finds her way back home. She becomes the hero of her own story. Later in the series of books written about the Land of Oz, she is named the Princess of Oz. Some of us surely dream of being a princess.

We all learn one way or the other that we must take charge of our own lives, for no one else can. We learn to make wise decisions in order to become the hero in our own story. We learn we must find our own true purpose to feel that we have finally found home.

It doesn't dawn on the Scarecrow that he has always had the brains to help others until he is honored with a piece of paper the Wizard proclaims is his diploma, honoring his knowledge. He then takes a position ruling over the Emerald City when the Wizard leaves the Land of Oz in his hot-air balloon.

We learn that the rusting Tin Man had always been kind and sensitive, but he finds his true purpose, ruling over the Winkies, only after his journey on the Yellow Brick Road, where he helped Dorothy overcome the wickedness of the Wicked Witch. Receiving a testimonial heart-shaped watch appears to be the only thing the Tin Man needed to realize he always had the power to find his heart's desire.

And even though he helps Dorothy reach the Emerald City safely, fighting off the hardships presented by the Wicked Witch, the Cowardly Lion also doesn't believe in himself or find his true purpose until he receives the Medal of Valor from the Wizard. Then he becomes the ruler of all the animals in the land.

The child with autism is also searching for purpose and, most of all, meaning in life. The parents of a child with autism are praying their son or daughter will find a place where he or she feels safe and valued. The teacher, therapist, scientist, and doctor are all passionate about supporting parents and their child as they find this thing called hope.

Keeping My Ruby Red Shoes Close

IN MY "ORDINARY WORLD," I was just someone's daughter, someone's sister, someone's granddaughter, someone's cousin or friend. I was just a little girl looking for where she fit, wondering if over the rainbow, like Dorothy, I would find my heart's desire. I think my having a mother who always thought I could do better and a father who always believed I either had what it took or could certainly find what I needed created the tension suggested in the first stage of my "Hero's Journey."

Just a reminder, the Hero's Journey is a pattern of narrative identified by the American scholar Joseph Campbell that appears in drama, storytelling, myth, religious ritual, and psychological development. It describes the typical adventure of the archetype known as the Hero, the person who goes out and achieves great deeds on behalf of a group or tribe or community.

The hero moves from her Ordinary World to her "Call to Adventure." She then enters "Crossing the Threshold" phase, which is followed by "Meeting the Mentor," "Tests of Allies and Enemies," and "The Approach" phases, then "The Ordeal," "The Reward," and "The Road Back." She finally experiences "The Resurrection" and "The Return to Elixir."

The film *The Miracle Worker* and my first babysitting job with Barry and Susan, the two deaf-mute children living across the street, shook me, as Joseph Campbell suggests in The Call to Adventure stage. I felt that the first call was to become someone like Annie Sullivan, Helen Keller's teacher, or someone like Barry and Susan's teachers, to help children to find their voices. To be honest, I believe this Call to Adventure would come several different times on my journey.

The Refusal of the Call stage was the time I needed to wait and grow into the first call, as a ten-year-old is not quite capable of problem-solving at the level required to be a teacher like Annie or knowing all the strategies and interventions required to support children with special needs.

I have experienced Meeting the Mentor throughout my life. The list is long. It includes my father, my mother, Annie Sullivan, Barry and Susan, and my professors at college. It includes Rusty and the other children with autism I first met while completing my clinical hours in the Speech and Language Clinic at Arizona State University. It includes Dr. Bernard Rimland, founder of the Autism Society of America, Dr. Patricia Kane, the mothers and fathers at the Kaplan Foundation, Oak Hill School, and Wings Learning Center. It includes all the many speakers of the Marin Autism Lecture Series and, of course, all my colleagues, especially Agnes, Yuni, and Laxmi, each unique individuals on the spectrum of autism, my brother, and, most of all, my three sons.

Each of those mentors provided wisdom, guidance, and advice to help me on my journey.

In the next stage on the Hero's Journey, called Crossing the Threshold, the hero leaves the Ordinary World and enters a new region of unfamiliar rules and values. I truly believe that I crossed the threshold when I opened my first school, the Kaplan Foundation. This was certainly a new region for me. I was expected to lead. I was depended on to provide for the safety of children with very special needs 24/7. I was expected to make the difference in the lives of children, families, and employees. As Joseph Campbell points out, people aren't familiar with all the new rules and values at this stage, and neither was I.

Tests of Allies and Enemies, the next stage on the Hero's Journey, certainly helped me build courage, expand knowledge, and lead with my heart. There were those who questioned my dream of opening a school. There were financial challenges to consider. There were rules and regulations and policies and procedures to develop and implement. There were state agencies looking for faults. There were agencies refusing to pay, insurance companies denying, and faculty and staff with less than good intentions, but each time I was able to find solutions. There were also friends, colleagues, and family along the way to support and help and believe in the possibility.

"The Approach" is a stage I am not so clear on. This is said to be a time when the hero and his or her new allies prepare for a major challenge. Maybe this was my getting through my mother's death with support from my father and brother. Maybe this was my getting over the first time my husband had an affair, my three sons' lives each teaching me what is truly important, and finally learning forgiveness, a key ally in life.

Then came the Ordeal stage—unbelievable. This is when the hero touches bottom and is said to be facing death, fighting a mythical beast. According to Joseph Campbell, this is a critical time, a chance to be born again. I can only tell you that the Ordeal stage seemed to go on for some time, as I thought I had touched bottom, only to realize that more was to come and that I was going to be asked to fight the beast again and again, and stand back up each time.

The final time my husband had an affair—the death of my marriage— was the first beast I had to overcome. Then came the loss of the Kaplan Foundation, which was another type of death to be overcome for it was the death of a child's longtime dream. Then, with my need to move out of Sacramento and take a leadership position at Oak Hill School in Marin County, the loss of seeing my youngest son every day. Finally, the very bottom for sure, a loss of unconditional love—the loss of my father on December 1, 2005.

How can one not change and not be different after so much loss?

But then comes the next stage, The Reward. If wisdom is a reward, then I have lived the Reward stage. If finding strength and expanding my knowledge and knowing I could continue to make a difference, then I have felt the Reward stage. Losing the Kaplan Foundation gave me the opportunity to spend time with my father in his last years of life. That was a reward. Helping a school for emotionally challenged students in Sacramento to develop and expand was my reward of self-esteem. Helping four families successfully create Oak Hill School in Marin was my reward of knowledge. Finally, going on to meet the needs of the North Bay Area community by creating the Marin Autism Lecture Series and North Bay Autism Resources Fair was the reward of courage to try something no one had.

The Road Back, the next stage on the Hero's Journey, represents possibly leaving the Adventure and returning to the Ordinary World. I see this stage reflected in the time I took off after directing Oak Hill School for six years. I needed time to process the Ordeal and Reward stages and to determine what part of The Road Back I wanted to choose. Traveling, teaching in the university system, developing educational opportunities all provided insight into what the road back might look like.

In The Resurrection, the eleventh stage, the hero emerges once again in the Ordinary World. Some say this is a rebirth of some kind. What I can tell you about this stage for me was that Agnes's mentorship in Thinking Bigger and my time spent outside the Ordinary World brought me right back on the road and rekindled my life's dream of directing a school. Taking on Wings Learning Center and helping the center take its rightful place in the community of autism reenergized my return. But completing seven years of helping in Indonesia was really about the rebirth and transformation of my journey.

The final stage of the Hero's Journey, the Return to Elixir, suggests that each of us continues on our own special journey. Having gone through all those previous stages, we now go on, transformed forever by the lessons we have learned and treasures we have acquired.

My treasures going forward:

> We all have come into this world with a purpose, and our journey is to find out what it is.

> Unconditional love of a parent, brother, son, daughter, and friend is truly the most meaningful part of life.

> While it is wonderful that others believe in us, we must believe in ourselves.

> Loss is devastating, but we must pick ourselves up and believe we will be okay.

> Failure is not in losing something but in not finding other ways to make a difference.

> Be honest, do not destroy hope, and do not judge.

> Forgive.

> Teach, mentor, leave a legacy.

I know my journey on my Yellow Brick Road is not over. I also know exactly where to find my ruby red shoes. I am always ready for the next Call to Adventure

I suggest you, too, keep your Ruby Red Slippers, your boots, stilettos, or pumps in tip-top condition and in a ready position for your Call to Adventure. The world needs heroes.

Hope Begins Even in the Title of a Book

As you know, I have written this book to inspire hope. So, let me draw you, the reader, to a simple point of view. Hope is evident in the history of the books written and published on autism.

In the '70s, when I first started buying books on autism, the selection was limited and fear, sadness, and hopelessness seemed to be the message in those titles: *Children Apart* by Dr. Lorna Wing, *Nobody Nowhere* by Donna Williams, *The Siege* by Clara Claiborne Park, *The Ultimate Stranger* by Dr. Carl H. Delacato, *Empty Fortress* by Bruno Bettelheim, and *The Wild Boy of Aveyron* by Dr. Jean Itard.

Then, all of a sudden the titles changed and the number of books published skyrocketed. *A Miracle to Believe In* by Dr. Barry Neil Kaufman gave hope. *Somebody Somewhere* by Donna Williams was encouraging. *Overcoming Autism* by Lynn Kern Koegel and Claire LaZebnik helped. *Label Me Jeff: A Special Kind of Normal* by Carolyn Betts had a parent sharing hopefulness. *Succeeding with Autism: Hear My Voice* by Judith Cohen was positive, and *Love, Hope and Autism* by Joanna Edgar was not fearful to pick up. *Laughing and Loving with Autism*, compiled by R. Wayne Gilpin, surely had smile potential for its readers.

Please enjoy this extensive bibliography on autism filled with hopefulness at: http://www.autism-resources.com/autism-bib.html. Hundreds of books and curriculums and papers are available. Check out the titles. Choose the hopeful ones.

See other resources on my websites: www.karenkaplanasd.com and www.globalofferings.org.

Karen's Emeralds

THE EMERALD CITY WAS SAID to have been made of the finest green marble and studded with giant sparkling emeralds. The brightness of the glimmering emeralds dazzled everyone in the Land of Oz. They certainly brightened the path enabling Dorothy to find her way.

A friend and colleague of mine suggested that I include some of my life's gems at the end of this story. Some believe that the emerald is the symbol of hope and that it brings reason and wisdom. It is my hope that perhaps one of them brings a bit of brightness, like the glimmering emeralds on the gates to the Emerald City, on your journey. So here are thirteen of my emeralds.

- Do not be possessed by your possessions.

- Breathe deeply both in and out.

- Let go of what you cannot control.

- Education and experience lay a strong foundation for success.

- Do not fear reaching out and asking.

- Life is a balance of using your Knowledge, Heart, and Courage.

- Think Bigger.

- Be grateful.

- Believe in your own strengths.

- Find yourself mentors.

- Secure your own life mask first.

- Take time to pause, look inside, and assess before choosing your direction.

- You will find home many times in your life, in places and in people you meet on the road.

Epilogue

I alone cannot change the world, but I can cast a stone across the waters to create many ripples.

~ *Mother Teresa*

I PLAN TO CONTINUE CASTING stones in the water to help others. I plan to continue making journeys to other cultures that are open to learning and collaborating. I plan to write my next book outlining in detail how to start a successful school for children with autism. I plan to work collaboratively with other like-minded individuals to create opportunities for those with unique capabilities.

I will continue to believe in capabilities instead of disabilities, possibilities instead of scarcity, and hope instead of despair.

My ruby red shoes will be right by my side for a long, long time.

About the Author

KAREN KAPLAN has been founding and directing schools for children with autism since 1980. She has special education and administrative credentials and a master's in speech pathology. In June of 2012, she founded a nonprofit organization, Offerings, which takes her to other cultures where she helps those who want to understand individuals with autism and other developmental challenges. She is currently the executive director at Wings Learning Center, a school for children with autism, in Redwood City, California, and consults with families, schools, and centers. She lives in Marin County. Her proudest moments are those she shares with her three adult sons.

Connect with Karen at www.karenkaplan.com
or karensupportsu@comcast.net.